OUR TURN TO POLLUTE

Ronald Rwakigumba

To my lovely parents, Rosemary and Joseph
Ever indulging me in critical thinking, open mindedness and adventure, never minding my mistakes, in fact, almost celebrating the consequences of such indulgence, even into murky futures

PREFACE

The world as we know it is changing in a multi faceted way and fast. Various facets of the change are demanding our attention creating a pressure on prioritization already. How then can we be discussing sustainability which intrinsically calls for optimizing various facets of the ongoing change.

Businesses at present are grappling with maintaining effective shareholder engagement and ensuring the best return possible. The current philosophy of most business is that shareholders having invested financial resources in the business undertaking hold residual risk and as such the obligation to align residual risk with reward.
At the same time businesses are considering impacts of finite and scarce resources needed in the productions of goods and services. In an increasing globalised world, the opportunity for a global market comes with complexity of global sourcing and sales supply chains. More so at present with the ongoing Covid-19 pandemic.

But we know now that other stakeholders beyond shareholders can also experience residual risk from operations of companies. They may not be investors whose shares risk plummeting from company operations but could be citizens perhaps living close to their production facilities and bearing the waste management ecological impacts. It therefore follows that such stakeholder also should be considered given the residual risk they are likely to experience. The triple bottom line is one of the globally accepted frameworks to guide companies to balance profit, people, and planet.

Countries are continuing to pursue growth and development and the narrative of least developed countries being a source of both supply of raw materials and demand for processed goods is starting to change. Increased emphasis on value addition processes, industrialization, and local content creation is creating jobs, and improving the balance of payments position of countries through increased exports. Globally this form of improvement of Gross Domestic Product has come with increase in greenhouse gas emissions.

The gains realized in jobs, exports, innovation risk being watered away by destructive climatic events like extreme floods, prolonged drought. These climate change induced events disproportionately impact least developed countries whose population is mostly employed in agriculture with less adaptation to modern farming methods like irrigation or improved farming inputs to shelter the impact.

Many a time when faced with this challenge of balancing development with ecological goals, some have argued that industrialization is the opportunity of least developing countries, whose turn it is now to pollute the environment just as developed countries did for many decades. Other countries have also argued that they still have what to pollute unlike developed states that apparently are overpopulated and at ecosystem breaking points. The irony I see is that developed states which are increasingly seeking to decouple GDP growth from GHG increase in emissions are also the most prepared to withstand extreme climatic events.

There must be another way for growth at either lesser increase in pollution or even decoupling altogether.

The aim of this book is to chart this other path of green industry which encompasses aspects of resource efficiency and reduced pollution providing insights on decoupling GDP growth from

GHG increase.

Another aim of the book is to support executives in navigating this broadened responsibility for social and environment needs and how triple bottom line can be satisfied as a help for shareholder and board approvals for investments made for ecological and social responsibilities.

Greening Industry and Corporate social responsibility while not new, this book focussed on providing solutions and ways in which companies and governments can navigate these aims. The arguments for the goals are also as important to win -over more executives equipping them with tools to innovate for various industries. A native of Uganda, East Africa, I aim to convince other African nations and fellow citizens of our shared home Earth, that it is not our turn to pollute using an antiphrasis title. Sustainability requires many actors to come together and this book is an attempt to connect the different actor experiences to facilitate as they embark on their sustainability journeys.

This book was written during a very creative period when I was exposed to leading industry experts during my pursuit of the Green Energy and Sustainable Businesses MBA, later work in Rome and short trainings in Trieste, Milan, Brussels, Lugano on sustainability related topics. It was also a hungry time for answers about the untenability of business as usual. What really helped in exploring both the question and solutions was a valuable comfort with being wrong. This ability to be comfortable with going into dead ends or assumptions being wrong reduced the barriers to learning.

There is also value that the book initially collected 'digital dust' on hard drives since 2013 when some of the last entries were written to the present time in 2020. The time that passed gave me more context and maturity when editing not necessarily to dilute the passion but channel and sequence the chapters better. The seven year gap was also an opportunity to step away from conferences, academic debates and step into practice realm where I literally picked up the tools and worked with communities to solve problems in a way that I hope advanced system and localised change and make great friendships int he process. It's these later year 7years that both enriched the structure of this book but also increased the urgency to publish it in these challenging times.

We speak of companies, countries and sometimes we almost forget we are also individuals. These discussions of sustainability also matter for us at an individual level. In fact, I originally wrote this literacy as a personal compass to refer to as I was working on various development projects.

I hope this book gives executives a second thought before measuring, reporting CSR to incorporate a fuller and change making approach. And while they do that, I also hope the public whom as stakeholders with substantial residual risk hold companies to a higher standard or at least ask more difficult questions to provide the checks expected as stakeholders. The notion that companies exist to serve only shareholder interests is challenging given non-shareholder stakeholders also bare residual risk and, in some sectors, perhaps greater residual risk.

The pursuit of answers on a Camelot-like equilibrium of people planet profit was a major motivating factor, however my jigsaw still does not fit. I hope this invites you and other passionate discoverers to mend the jigsaw. In fact, it is to these relentless future sustainability scholars and those before us that I dedicate this work.

CONTENTS

Title Page

Copyright

Dedication

Preface

Sustainability   1

Pricing the Environment   15

Climate Inaction   35

Green Energy & SDGs   57

Sustainable Development   83

About The Author   115

SUSTAINABILITY

"The future is already here – it's just not evenly distributed."

WILLIAM GIBSON

Sustainability's complexity rather than discourage, could motivate us to start, as Plato would say, "the beginning is the most important work". One may ask, what makes sustainability so complex? Perhaps because it seeks to make an optimum of social, environment, and economic spheres that intrinsically struggle to reach their individual optimum. A system of systems.

There seems to be a need of a comprehensive internationally accepted definition of sustainability. That might sound ambitious but we need the definition, at least for as long as we use the very word to transfer meaning across cultures and communities whom at present have another interpretation. To begin the journey to such a definition, I provide the key ingredients of such a definition.

A discussion of Sustainability would be incomplete without an analysis of Corporate Social Responsibility (CSR) reporting. *'Are the World's Most Sustainable Companies really Sustainable?'* I explain how Companies have succeeded in sustaining ambiguity around the format of CSR reports; others have gone on to use their own formats. It is peculiar that a function which informs us on how resources have been utilized, distributed and how they impact the ecosystem is left with such insurmountable ambiguity. Accounting on the other hand, which is an offspring of how those resources and factors of production are applied, has clear International Accounting standards. No company comes to the end of the financial year without duly prepared and in some cases audited financial statements, yet the underpinning function that generate that very financial performance are only a subsequent consideration.

Also providing useful insights into Green Strategy, comparing sustainability and clean energy aspirations with the existing demand implications. Somethign that permiates almost all chapters is the aspect of practical solutions or actionable knowledge. Like Herbert Spencer (1820-1903) who said that

the great aim of education is not knowledge but action.

Pursuing a Definition

The wallpaper on my desktop is the last monastery I visited in the Le Marche region of Italy - Monastero dei Frati Bianchi. It is not the renovated building that intrigue me, but rather the caves where the monks used to live in search of a higher enlightenment as they also prayed for a good harvest. The monks do not live here anymore, I respectfully walked in the little path leading here engulfed in the woods amidst pin drop silence. Occasionally that silence was pleasantly interrupted by the little streams on the sides that are a shadow of their past when they might have been gushing large waters.

I do not have the answer to the question of what the Latin word 'sustinere' means, and the monks would not be too disappointed, for the beginning of all quests is in asking questions.

One approach to define Sustainability is looking at it's causes and effects as seen in the Australian Curriculum v5.1 when defining sustainability, reads *'Sustainability addresses the ongoing capacity of Earth to maintain all life.'*

The Sustainability Consortium approaches a definition by looking at the rational *'Increasingly pressure is being felt by multiple stakeholders to reduce the environmental and social impacts associated with global consumption.'* Think tank SustainAbility identifies two ways of defining Sustainability; *'Among the many ways that sustainability has been defined, the simplest and most fundamental is: "the ability to sustain" or, put another way, "the capacity to endure."*

These are examples of defining Sustainability by explaining the challenges of the status quo and how sustainability is a necessary consideration.

Could the question of *'what is Sustainability?'* be rephrased as *'what is your definition of Sustainability?'* since different people define sustainability differently? The Citizens Network for Sustainable Development mentions that *'Depending on who you are and what you find important, your definition or concept of sustainability will likely vary from others —* assuming you have one.' They go on to say that sustainability is not alone in ambiguity, since *'words such as truth, justice, love, freedom, faith, have multiple and often conflicting definitions.'*

It is possible to extract meaning of Sustainability from the definition of Sustainable Development. The 1987 definition of Sustainable development by the World Commission on Environment and Development (the Brundtland Commission) has to-date received the widest acceptance. The commission defined Sustainable Development as

> *'development that meets the needs of the present without compromising the ability of future generations to meet their own needs'*

One can extract the Sustainability definition as *'the ability to meet the needs of the present without compromising the ability of future generations to meet their own needs'*

Why should we bother so much about the future? Charles Kettering has an answer, as he notes;

> *'My interest is in the future because I am going to spend the rest of my life there.'*

He also encourages us with the thought that, *'there will always be a frontier where there is an open mind and a willing hand'*

Although we seem to agree on passing on *'something'* to the future generations, it is not clear what exactly we should preserve. Should we preserve every living and nonliving thing? And how sure are we future generations need what we are passing on? Papyrus used to be used for writing, horses for transportation etc. But we've moved on 'for better or for worse' to use paper and cars respectively. What we might value less today, could be tomorrow's treasure, and perhaps we might be preserving things future generations have no need for since we do not know what will shape tomorrow with certainty. A key ingredient for sustainability is the perspective of regeneration of renewable resources, while planning for substitution of non-renewable resources.

Efficiency is similarly a key tenet of sustainability as future generation demand of us to be as waste-free as possible today. Then again, sustainability is not only about saving for the future, it is also about the present, about employees working healthy hours, about safety at workplaces, about safe delivery by mothers world wide, about provision of education, about observing human rights, and not being selective as to which rights to enforce. Sustainability is about welfare, and making sure that welfare is enjoyed sensibly, efficiently, and considerately.

Sustainability is complex because it seeks to make an optimum of spheres that in themselves, individually struggle to reach their optimum. A system of systems. Take for instance, in the Economic sphere, to maximise profit, one can attempt to reduce costs of production, increase sales, or find better rewarding vehicles of investment. Not only does each of these have tensions but can affect other spheres like Social and Environment objectives. For example, one might reduce staffing and create a social challenge, or cut costs in waste management and generate environmental challenges.

It is already complex enough to optimize social, environment, or economic objectives individually, therefore one can only imagine how daunting it must be to achieve sustainability, whose purpose is to simultaneously reconcile all three for better present and future welfare, meaningful and lasting welfare, thus the term 'sustainable development'

Yet Plato tells us to start for

"*the beginning is the most important work*"

Plato could easily be misunderstood to be saying that one must dwell on perfecting the start. It is impossible to perfect the beginning, as almost everything is a work in progress, and therefore Plato must have been referring to something else.

I think Plato wanted to bring to light the power of beginning. The courage, zeal to begin any work is the most important thing, because once something has been started it has the power within it to grow, self-correct, and birth other beginnings. Some have termed it as seeding, and we know what happens to a good seed planted in a conducive environment.

But Plato seems to be telling us something more than a beginning. When we think of planting a seed, we also start to think of the soils, of the moisture, nutrients. By giving the beginning such importance, Plato is reminding us that to germinate, the beginning needs to be nourished.

Sustainability is already having many beginnings, different beginnings, and the journey itself might seem difficult, but if we focus on these sprouting beginnings, we might get the work done right, the most important work.

After various edits, I now define Sustainability as

> *the means by which human nature thrives in achieving fulfillment as a consequence of applying natural and man-made factors of production whilst ensuring regeneration of renewable resources and planning for the substitution of non-renewable resources to the extent that social considerations, Innovation, technology permit.*

It is a journey.

Beyond Sustainability, Transparency

Intel's Rio Rancho Facility (New Mexico, USA) publicly makes available information on the plant's use of water, waste, energy, and air pollution over the web. Environmental Information provided includes Water Conserved, Water Used, Percent Non-Hazardous Waste Recycled, Non-Hazardous, Waste Generated, Percent Hazardous Waste to Landfill, Hazardous Waste Generated, Electricity Saved (kWh), Electricity Generated from Solar, Greenhouse Gas (GHG) Emissions, Volatile Organic Compounds (VOC), and Hazardous Air Pollutants (HAPs) in rare show of transparency.

In this rare show of transparency and with growing green conscious consumers, Intel could easily be turning sustainability into a new competitive edge through transparency, probably a new frontier for differentiation.

Corporate sustainability reporting has its challenges, as it can be difficult to trust that what companies are reporting is factual, and one can be weary of companies reporting only aspects that reflect well on them. The CSR function is becoming another costume companies parade to show us how good they are looking in the sphere of sustainability.

Evaluating the sustainability of a company depends on the sector, and as such each sector has specific guidelines. It then requires a variety of matrices if one company is involved in diverse market offerings and processes. For my sector level analysis, I will use Version 3.0 of the internationally respected Key Performance Indicators for Environmental, Social & Governance Issues (KPIs for ESG. A Guideline for the Integration of ESG into Financial Analysis and Corporate Valuation).

These guidelines are endorsed by the European Federation of Financial Analysts Society (EFFAS) and Society of Investment Professionals in Germany (DVFA). source.

For example, Companies in the Materials Technology Sector of Catalysis, Energy provide a variety of Environment, Social and Economic metrics (ESG). On their Global Reporting Initiative (GRI)index, one can find Direct energy consumption by primary energy source; Indirect energy consumption by primary energy source; Energy saved due to conservation and efficiency improvements; Initiatives to provide energy-efficient or renewable energy based products and services; and Initiatives to reduce indirect energy consumption, and reductions achieved.

Providing information and environmental performance are not the same thing. For example, one firm's energy consumption between 2010 and 2011 increased from 7,597 TJ to 7,807 TJ. The justification for this increase is the rise in revenues by 15% which is greater than the increase in energy consumption of 3%.

However, sustainability requires a decoupling of growth in Energy consumption from growth in revenue through energy efficiency. It is a given that production, or revenue growth which are not necessarily related will happen to meet demand, however this growth should not necessarily result in energy consumption increase if sustainability goals are to be met and an energy crisis averted. It is for this reason that industries need to be 'greened'.

It comes as no surprise that the same firm's CO_2e emissions (scope1+2) (in tonne) grew from 513,807 in 2010 to 695,733 in 2011. Again, growth in revenues is moving with increase in CO_2 emissions. This is the same phenomenon that happened in the EU (27) (2008 – 2010) when less production meant that companies naturally emitted less for the most part without having to put in place energy efficiency measures, but rather, as a consequence of the economic crisis which shrunk demand and national GDP growth.

Worth acknowledging the significant, and perhaps unprecedented effort in publicly providing this information including revealing the total investments in research on ESG relevant aspects of business.

However, areas for improvement exist. I couldn't find information on Average expenses on training per Full Time Employees (FTE), p.a; and a Key Performance Narrative to find out whether the company integrates ESG principals within performance agreements.

Ambiguity and varied formats of CSR report do not lend well to comparison within sectors and it's peculiar that a function which informs us on how resources have been utilized, distributed and how they impact the ecosystem is left with such insurmountable ambiguity. Accounting on the other hand, which is an offspring of how those resources and factors of production are applied, has clear International Accounting standards.

We understand sustainability, at least enough to draft rules and guidelines for corporate entities to follow. It is a serious failure of markets and stock exchange regulations for the core substance and value creations processes to go unregulated. No company comes to the end of the financial year without duly prepared and audited financial statements, yet the underpinning function that generate that very financial performance are only a subsequent consideration.

Ethical consideration for Sustainability.

Sarah, in Kampala, paid six months' rent for a house she thought had piped water. The confidence of the brokers, and ambiguity of the landlord's representative, led her not to question whether water indeed flows from the taps. Even when she turned on the tap and water didn't flow, she assumed it was a temporary intermittent supply. Eventually when Sarah moved-in her house to find no running water, the landlord informed her the broker should have told her, which the broker denies say it is a shame the landlord never told her.

But Sarah has never met the landlord; she only met his representative - Tom, whom apparently under strict instructions was not to disclose the matter of running water under the agency relationship with his master. Tom says he is a moral person, and works transparently, arguing that on this occasion he was only acting on instructions from his master the landlord.

Obedience to Authority & Agentic state can cause individuals to perform harmful acts without a tinge of regret since they perceive themselves as merely agents, acting for others.

Agentic state theory observes that a person comes to view themselves as the instrument for carrying out another person's wishes, and they therefore no longer see themselves as responsible for their actions. Once this critical shift of viewpoint has occurred in the person, all the essential features of obedience follow. Therefore, individuals are not likely to consider sustainability issues if they perceive their actions as those of another, and only acting as agents.

Closely related to this agentic behavior is the theory of conformism which explains the challenge posed by individuals trying to conform to groups of reference. If someone has neither the ability nor the expertise to make a decide, especially in a crisis, they will leave decision making to the group and its hierarchy. The group assumes the person's behavioral model.

To effectively address the sustainability challenge, we need to recognize that it is not just individual behavior and decisions we are dealing with, but also group actions & decisions.

Some argue that we are neither ethical nor unethical, we are merely Amoral, only doing what shareholders want, and the market expects.

Starting with shareholders' interests as new moral yardstick. If business is Amoral, then is the shareholder also amoral? I doubt. If the stakeholder is moral, then by extension the business has a prerogative in representing the shareholder, and thus an obligation to be moral, too.

Executives often choose to willfully be blind to the improper actions, culture, behavior that ultimately not only leads to the collapse of corporations, but ruin very many lives.

Sustainability and Ethics are in effect a story about people, because unethical behavior is capable of not only hurting others, but eroding from the perpetrators their very moral compass, such that it is difficult to distinguish between the victim and the 'smart guy'.

Story of the Batwa - Uganda

When I visited the Batwa community in Bwindi - South Western Uganda they told me a fable of their 'misfortune' on finding when the 'Creator' had given away when almost all the riches in the world to other tribes and people. As the tale goes, they all that was left were forests, which as the only resource left was taken by the Batwa who became 'Keepers of the Forest'.

That fate was to change when they were evicted from Bwindi Forest to protect the habitat of Gorilla and other wildlife calling Bwindi Impenetrable Forest home. The Batwa who had co-existed with the Gorillas and other wild animals for ages now found themselves evicted from Bwindi Impenetrable Forest paradoxically because they were perceived to be a threat to the Gorillas.

When the Batwa were removed, Good Samaritan's like Dr. Scott and Carol Kellermann supported the Batwa in land acquisition with over 300 acres of land purchased, for their settlement in the Buhoma side of Bwindi. Ironically the Gorillas frequently visit the Batwa new location – in fact so much so that those tracking the gorillas sometimes have to use the paths created by the Batwa so as to access Gorillas on those occasions when they are near the Batwa residence in Buhoma. The elders told me Gorillas are social, they love people. Dr. Scott Kellermann went on to found the Bwindi Community Hospital with over 112 beds to provides healthcare to the entire Bwindi area among other efforts like education, under the Batwa Development Program.

A portion of the proceeds from Gorrila tourist activities in Bwindi is sent back to the local community to support Batwa development programs. Somethings money and development programs can't compensate. Dignity. They lost their language, even the remaining elders do not speak it anymore, the knowledge of treating various ailment with local herbs might also have disappeared. Their culture is waiting to die with only a few people are holding it together. Their religion is not practiced – even the faith in their god (Abasinga) has deteriorated. When I was departing, I wished the elders that Abasinga keeps them well, to my surprise one elder responded –

"the Abasinga is no longer powerful – must have abandoned us."

Social initiatives like Batwa Development Program thrive from business models that create revenue e.g. through cultural education, sale of artifacts, donation programs which is then ploughed back to sustain and continue alleviating the challenges communities like the Batwa experience.

Earlier, while attending a Social Business Conference at Universita della Svizzera Italiana's Aula Magna, in Lugano Switzerland, dozens of questions crisscrossed my mind. Nobel Peace Prize Laureate Professor Muhammad Yunus delivering his keynote speech was inspiring with perfect unscripted choice of words charismatically speaking with purpose, and vision.

Social businesses have a special part to play in providing sustainable solutions to community challenges. It is foreseeable for social enterprises to be limited to addressing problems whose commercialization is plausible as part of a dependence on a viable model that can be developed. Who will address the social and environment problems that cannot be commercialized? And, as social businesses are addressing today's problems, who will address problems being created today whose manifestation will be tomorrow? who shall address the salient problems?

What I learn from the Batwa is that the world is about a cake being distributed. Some want more of it and will do anything to have it, ethical or unethical. But I also learn of humanity's self-healing power – that there are social innovators who discomfort themselves to correct a social wrong and alleviate suffering.

Lord Nicholas Stern's comments best engulf the happenings thus far *"This is potentially so dangerous that we have to act strongly. Do we want to play Russian roulette with two bullets or one? These risks for many people are existential."*
The path of business-as-usual is highly untenable.
Therefore, promoting sustainable girl child education requires a multi-pronged strategy: increasing access by removing the social, economic, cultural entry barriers; building a 'ring fence' through better collaboration between teachers and parents to reduce pregnancy related dropouts, but also 'electrifying' that ring fence through punitive measures to the male culprits involved in child pregnancy cases.

Up until this point, sustainability, and the direction of 'green energy' has been broadly received with more people embracing the concept of cleaner supply. We have gotten to the point where the innovators dilemma is less about convincing the market that they have the cleaner supply but rather providing the market with the capacity to run either as complementary or in substitution of the existing supply.

Now the solution to the innovator's dilemma seems to be on the one hand increasing efficiency in the solar industry, increase innovation in the wind turbine sector, but simultaneously partner with the less clean energy sources with the objective of sustainably increasing efficiency. The numbers deem these other sources are relevant, since in the next projected twenty years we need a good supply even of non renewable energy.

This partnership could solve the innovator's dilemma, emanating from a cocktail-like Sustainability model.

PRICING THE ENVIRONMENT

'A forest landowner does not get PAID for the services his forest provides to fishermen and farmers by protecting of soil against erosion and hydropower dams against sedimentation. Nor does s/he obtain commercial PROFITS for capturing carbon, maintaining scenic beauty or for preserving biodiversity resources. The forest landowner has little INCENTIVE to take these benefits into account and therefore the production of these environmental services will be less than if he could sell them and receive a FINANCIAL REWARD.'

ARNOLDO CONTRERAS-HERMOSILLA, IN 'THE UNDERLYING
CAUSES OF FOREST DECLINE'

W e can either live with the consequences of environmental degradation or pay for ecosystem services and save ourselves.

Although it is well known that the market has not attached a price on all valuable commodities and services, it is not that much known how in medieval times, subtle value attachment mechanisms boosted sustainability. When visiting the countryside of Urbino, Italy I found myself learning about doves, housewives, and sustainability. In the medieval era, apparently households loved doves because that was their major source of income, thus they cared and fed them diligently. Knowingly or unknowingly the market price of the doves ensured the survival and thriving of doves.

Curbing GHG emissions effectively will require attaching a price and various Emissions Trading systems (ETS) are emerging around the world to complement the EU ETS. Australia, Europe, China, Switzerland, State of California, Kazakhstan, Croatia, Quebec, South Africa, and a few South American countries already have a cap based, carbon tax, or emissions trading system already in place. However, the absence of legally binding commitments affects demand for credits from Carbon Market investors thus compromising efforts to proportionally respond to climate change.

As the households saved the doves and profited, even today environmental value could capture and catalyze good business model to generate value to keeping the ecosystem in balance.

Today, our doves are the environment, which when properly priced can correct the market system. Are the pricing mechanisms efficient, and effective? Not yet. However, the alternative is hardly that the world will make it cost nothing to pollute.

The growing environmental pollution can be curtailed through shifting to a more energy—efficient economy which can accelerate spread of innovative technologies, and improve competitiveness of industry, thus boosting economic growth and creating high quality jobs in several sectors. For the most part, controlling our impact on the environment is shrouded with imperfect information. For instance, afforestation programs are often used to justify tree felling for commercial purposes. The argument given is that the practice is carbon neutral since new planted trees compensate for those felled.

However 'carbon neutral' is not the same as 'ecosystem neutral' since little has been done to find ways to restore the affected animal diversity found in natural forests,

*which is hard to replicate once trees have been felled, and
which take years to restore, perhaps at times too little too
late and the animals have moved on, or died.*

'A Climate on Steroids'? In 2013, floods ravaged Australia leaving
at least four people dead in Queensland state and three dead in
Brisbane. In South America, 6 people died from record rains that
struck southern Peruvian town of Arequipa in February 2013, the
same month in which a Tsunami destroyed villages in Solomon
Islands. In the same year, other countries weren't spared floods
in Turkey, Mozambique, United Kingdom, Indonesia, Malaysia,
Kenya, Uganda, and China which has been experiencing a resur-
gence of floods. Tim Flannery, the then Chief Commissioner of
Australia's Bureau of Meteorology likened the weather to 'a climate on steroids' when referring to extreme weather events that
in some ways are like an athlete who improves their baseline performance by taking steroids.

> *"The analogy I like to use is an athlete on steroids. He or she
> is an athlete naturally, but if he or she is tempted to take
> steroids, they run faster and jump higher. So basically, we
> have a climate on steroids and the steroids are provided by
> the long underlying trend of global climate change."*

Decoupling GDP from GHG Emissions

The role of decoupling GDP growth from increase in emissions
could not have been more relevant today. The European economic
crisis not only stifled GDP growth across the region, but as a direct
result reduced production from falling demand with the domino
effect being fewer emissions by companies, perhaps one of few
'positives' to emanate from the crisis.

To understand the impact GDP triggered reduction in emissions has to the overall sustainability discussion, there is need to mention the second phase of the EU Emissions Trading System (ETS), 2008-2012. Under the 2008-2012 phase II, the emissions targets as per the Kyoto Protocol were used as a benchmark for providing EU Allowances (EUAs) to individual nations under the National Allocation Plans (NAPS), with emissions allowances being freely given to companies.

The direct result of less production meant that companies naturally emitted less for the most part without having to put in place energy efficiency measures, but rather, as a consequence of the credit crisis which shrunk demand and national GDP growth. Companies therefore sought to sell the excess emissions permits on the EU ETS thus increasing supply without necessary corresponding demand. The supply side was further increased by the carbon credits claimed through the Clean Development Mechanisms, Joint Implementation agreed in the Marrakesh Accords. Of course, the price of carbon permits fell drastically to below €5 (at present) from €30 per metric tonne of CO_2.

Such is the supply side of the challenge that on 25th July 2012 the EU commission on climate change proposed changes to the ETS directive allowing for Emissions Allowances to be auctioned as opposed to being freely given. Further still, the commission proposes to control supply by being given the mandate to alter the date when the auctions are made to avoid over supply. In fact, the commission on the same day announced a delay in the proposed 2013 auction to reduce the backlog of allowances on the market, with proposed dates indicating the first auctions could be as late as 2015.

The table below shows the 955 CO_2 Metric tonnes surplus of carbon credits over time (EUAs, CERs, and ERUs)

Build-up of a surplus of unused allowances 2008-2011, EU (in Metric tonnes)

	2008	2009	2010	2011	Total
Issued Allowances and used international credits	2076	2105	2204	2336	8720
Reported emissions	2100	1860	1919	1886	7765
Annual change of surplus allowances	-24	244	285	450	955

Source: Community Independent Transaction Log (CITL), compliance data 2011 as published on 2 May 2012, European Commission

Evidence of GGD and GHG coupling.

As per the table below, verified emissions reduced by 11% from 2008 to 2009, in part due to the falling GDP owing to the credit crisis. The emissions increased the following year by a less percentage of 3%, in part due to increasing GDP, only for the emissions to reduce in 2011, again in part due to falling GDP.

	2008	2009	2010	2011	Total
Verified emissions (in Mt)	2100	1860	1919	1886	7765
Change to year x-1		-11.4%	3.2%	-1.8%	
GDP (real growth rate EU27)	0.3%	-4.3%	2%	1.5%	

Source: Community Independent Transaction Log (CITL), Compliance data 2011 as published on 02/05/2012, European Commission. GDP data as reported on http://epp.eurostat.ec.europa.eu on 06/05/2012.

Therefore, there is need to decouple this relationship between GDP and GHG emissions. Energy Efficiency, and Innovation seem to be the twin prescription to achieve GDP growth whilst concurrently reducing GHG emissions.

Questions could be asked as to the actual impact the EU ETS is having on the reduction of the emissions, especially, if we look at both charts simultaneously rather than in isolation. However, the key question here is the cost of the ETS, and whether the investment could have yielded better tangible emissions reductions if invested in Energy efficiency and innovation.

Before any conclusion can be reached, it is worth mentioning that developing energy efficiency initiatives and launching such projects can be complicated and we are only learning how best to execute such projects. Innovation is costly, and increasingly investors are asking for investment in *proven technology*. For innovations to subsequently qualify as proven technology takes even a much longer time.

Not all environment improvement measures need to be attached to emissions trading. Companies have the potential t either create value from products at the end of their useful life or safely disposal of the waste generated. However, for as long as recycling does not generate net financial gains, companies will naturally avoid the burden by blaming various agents in the supply chain, notwithstanding the fact that radical innovation in R&D takes time.

Let's take the tyre manufacturing Industry which tries to balance consumer safety with environmental impact reduction. The two have implicit consequences on each other. Faced with this dogma, I attended the 2012 Pirelli International Conference on Sustainability, Consumer Safety & Road Safety in Milan. Later that day, it occurred to me that benefits of used tyres are meagre in contrast to costs of collecting them. Disposal of used tyres will vary from one country to another – depending on availability and scale of disposal infrastructure, regulation, and enforceability. The ideal solution would be for more investment in R&D to get ways of efficient recycling of tyres.

> *"To talk about sustainability today, means first of all talking about technologies allowing a constant improvement of the quality of our life"*

MARCO TRONCHETTI PROVERA

The task ahead is to act as antagonists to reverse the GDP-GHG emissions union.

Fixing the EU Emissions Trading System

The intervention of EU Commission on Climate Action changing the ETS directive, allowing for Emissions Allowances to be auctioned as opposed to being freely given to work effectively, the commission needed to control supply by being given the mandate to alter the date when the auctions are made to avoid over supply.

I hoped that the commission would succeed with the proposed delay in 2013 auction to reduce the backlog of allowances on the market, with proposed dates indicating the first auctions could be as late as 2015.

Unfortunately, although the auctions were adopted, the need to postpone the 2013 auction was not achieved; with the result that the early 2013 auction of EU carbon permits had to be cancelled on 18th January 2013, after bidding failed to reach the reserve level, further driving down prices of EU Allowances (EUAs) to a record low. The European Energy Exchange AG in Leipzig, Germany, failed to generate higher bids even after extending the sale by 15 minutes. Hence the Carbon auction cancelled due to knock-down prices.

Fixing the EU ETS requires a multifaceted approach:
Back-loading proposal. This is the most immediate intervention needed and Connie Hedegaard, European Commissioner for Climate Action at the time emphasized this in her comments of 24th January 2013 on recent developments in the European carbon market. Back-loading refers to postponing the auctioning of

900 million allowances from 2013-2015 to later in phase three of the EU emissions trading system (phase three runs from 2013 to 2020). The proposal to 'back-load' auction volumes in phase three, takes the form of a draft amendment to the EU ETS Auctioning Regulation which was submitted on 12 November 2012 to the EU Climate Change Committee. The back-loading does not affect the overall volume of allowances to be auctioned in phase three, only the distribution of auction volumes over the eight-year period (the 'auction time profile' 2013-2020).

"Annex II" contained in the draft amendment (page 3) of the Commission on Climate Action's proposal, shows the Adjustments to the volumes of allowances to be auctioned in 2013-2020 referred to in Article 10(2).

To interpret the "Annex II", the volume on the auction is proposed to be reduced by a total of 900 million allowances with 400, 300, 200 in 2013, 2014, and 2015 respectively. Now these allowances will be added back in the last two years of the phase three, i.e. 300, and 600 million allowances in 2019 and 2020 respectively. This is what is meant by the draft wording in the proposal which reads as below.

> *"The volume of allowances to be auctioned in a given year determined pursuant to the first or second subparagraphs of this paragraph in 2013-2015 shall be reduced by the quantity of allowances for the respective year set out in the second column of the table in the Annex II to this Regulation.*

The volume of allowances to be auctioned in a given year determined pursuant to the first or second subparagraphs of this paragraph in 2019 to 2020 shall be increased by the quantity of allowances for the respective year set out in the third column of the table in the Annex II to this Regulation." That draft Decision still requires approval by the European Parliament and Council."

Demand side interventions. The demand side interventions could include the proposed admission of Chemical, and Aluminium companies to join the Scheme, with Airlines joining in 2012. Already, European Commission has taken an important step for the aviation industry to join other economic sectors in the fight against climate change. Aviation became part of the EU's emissions trading system (EU ETS) from 2012.

I opine that the problem of the ETS goes much further than that. The absence of legally binding commitments affects demand for credits from Carbon Market investors thus compromising the whole system. I applaud the proposal by the EU to apply a single EU cap as opposed to decentralized caps which introduce excesses. I agree that the alternative to a well-functioning carbon market is hardly that the EU Member States will make it cost nothing to pollute – based on her piece on recent developments in the European carbon market.

The EU ETS can be fixed by using back-loading; growing the emissions network which has expanded to include oil rich Kazakhstan, Croatia, Quebec, and State of California joining world's carbon trading schemes effective 1st January 2013. Australia, Switzerland already have carbon trading schemes with Australia-EU on pathway towards fully linking Emissions Trading systems.

It is self-evident that we should not write-off the EU ETS. There is a huge task ahead and this is not the time to give up, in fact, we have a chance to improve the EU ETS by submitting our proposals via the Public Consultation on structural options to strengthen the EU Emissions Trading System.

Curbing Aviation Emissions

It's not all doom and gloom. In suggestions to fixing the EU Emissions Trading System above, I mention how the European

Commission took an important step for the aviation industry to join other economic sectors in the fight against climate change. Achieved by including emissions from international aviation in the EU Emissions Trading System (EU ETS) and imposing a cap on CO_2 emissions from flights arriving at or departing from EU airports. This was the beginning of more challenges since the question of double taxation arise in the case of airlines arriving in the EU airports having been 'already' taxed in their country of origin.

However, had the EU not moved in first instance to provide a cap we would not be having the argument of how to treat the arrivals in the EU, and also how the EU departures will be treated on arrival on foreign soil.

When China announced in February 2012 it had banned its airlines from paying European Union charges on carbon emissions, some perceived this as escalating the issue of airline emissions, but as sustainability is a journey we should remember that this was a challenge on level two, with level one being that we had globally accepted that we had to do something about curbing the airlines emissions. Now, thanks to the move by the EU we had moved to level two of asking the how's and where's. Having a discussion of how much tax or cap to impose and where the cap or tax is applied and recognized. Therefore, this is indeed welcome in furthering the discussion towards an effective mechanism to address the aviation industry's climate pollutions.

Greenhouse gas emissions from airplanes are no small matter: if the aviation industry were a country, it would be the seventh largest emitter in the world.

What appears to be a practical solution to the impasse is provided by the EU's Climate Action, in which

> 'Incoming flights can be exempted from the EU ETS if the EU recognizes that the country of origin is taking measures to limit aviation emissions from departing flights.'

Since only a few countries are moving to curb climate change impact from the aviation industry, the EU had no alternative other than to apply the legislation on only flights within and between the European countries in the EU ETS whilst seeking a global agreement to tackle aviation emissions through the International Civil Aviation Organization (ICAO). This decision was accepted by the European Parliament.

How do we resolve the Aviation emissions' Cap and/or tax Impasse? First, we need to acknowledge the severity of aviation pollution. The EU Climate commission estimates that;

> *"Someone flying from London to New York and back generates roughly the same level of emissions as the average person in the EU does by heating their home for a whole year."*

A Manchester Metropolitan University report *'Bridging the aviation CO2 emissions gap: why emissions trading is needed'* authored by D.S. Lee, L.L. Lim and B. Owen shows that international aviation emissions which were 630Mtonnes CO2 in 2006 are projected to increase to between 1000 to 3,100Mtonnes CO2 by 2050. Thus, an increase of 392pc.

The necessary second step is to move towards a global Aviation Emissions Trading system. And this can be implemented given that leading markets in Australia, Europe, China, Switzerland, State of California, Kazakhstan, Croatia, Quebec, South Africa, and a few South American countries already have a cap based, carbon tax, or emissions trading system already in place. International air travel is globalized by default and to even attempt to address a problem of this scale we need a global perspective and approach.

Correcting market failures. Not pricing the climate emissions by airlines is a market failure. There is a cost to the environment, but this cost has not been priced into the operations of airlines.

When people are comparing transportation prices, they rarely price in these externalities. For example, trains and other Cleaner transportation vessels do not receive extra revenues for being cleaner and good for the environment. Instead they must compete in an imperfect market system with other less clean transportation modes. A global cap and/or tax on Aviation emissions will not only spur humanity towards solving other challenges that require a worldwide view but will curb emissions from an industry that is important to all of us, and which we now invite to join in combating global climate change.

Commercial implications. From the business and consumer perspective, the implication to be monitored is with regard to whether airlines will cover these costs out of their revenues or they will pass on this cost to consumers, and if so, the magnitude of the cost passed on.

My undergrad research report on this topic, titled *'Inflation and Pricing Power of firms (2007)'* aimed to investigated the extent to which firms (such as Airline companies) pass on costs to customers in form of high prices, explaining the circumstances and forces that govern and influence this behavior with corresponding consumer reactions. The relevance of the study is for firms as they plan and design their pricing strategy to consider the degree of acceptability of their price and ability to achieve the expected revenue. Previous studies had identified a significant decline in the degree to which firms' pass-through costs to customers in prices, a decline characterized as a reduction in pricing power of firms.

New Market Mechanisms (NMM)

What are New Market Mechanisms? This is a question I wanted answered and on failing to find a satisfactory answer I embarked on a study to understand the rationale of having New Market

Mechanisms (NMM) when we had Clean Development Mechanisms (CDM) and Joint Implementation (JI) enshrined in the Kyoto Mechanisms of the United Nations Framework Convention on Climate Change (UNFCCC).

New Market Mechanisms (NMM) are a step forward towards climate change mitigation and come in to address the shortcomings observed with CDM and JI. Under Kyoto Mechanisms a developed country that undertakes a climate change mitigating project in a developing country earns Certified Emissions Reductions (CER), in what is termed as a Clean Development Mechanism (CDM). However, when a developed country undertakes a climate change mitigating project in another developed country, they earn Emissions Reduction Units (ERU), in what is termed as Joint Implementation (JI). Thus, it is common for NMM to be referred to as Post-Kyoto Mechanisms.

New Market Mechanisms (NMMs) are sector-based mechanisms in which national governments voluntarily set emissions benchmarks or baselines for an entire economic sector. In so doing national government earn credits for going beyond the emissions reductions required to meet this benchmark, thus the term 'sectoral crediting'. There are no binding obligations to meet the benchmarks and as a result the NMM baselines are often regarded as "no-lose" targets. For NMM to be effective in combating climate change, it is proposed that the emissions reductions achieved up to the no-lose target would not result in credits being created.

To ensure that meaningful targets are set, national baselines are encouraged to be below the Bali Action Plan (BAP) considerations. BAP provides for "nationally appropriate mitigation actions by developing country Parties in the context of sustainable development, supported and enabled by technology, financing and capacity-building, in a measurable, reportable and verifiable manner" (UNFCCC, 2008).

Benefits of New Market Mechanisms. The immediate benefit is the sectoral approach as opposed to the project-based implementation of the Kyoto Mechanisms. This will promote coordinated and effective climate mitigation action by individual nations that voluntarily set their baselines for sectoral emissions reductions. A salient benefit is the fact that developing countries will champion their own climate mitigation actions as opposed to dwelling so much on developed country interventions in form of clean development mechanisms. This will increase the scale of global climate mitigation by encouraging developing countries to take on greater mitigation commitments by enhancing the cost-effectiveness of mitigation action.

NMMs promote implementation of Nationally Appropriate Mitigation Actions (NAMAs) since national governments decide how to encourage emissions reduction in their sectors. Localization is an equitable way of addressing climate change, and therefore individual nations should decide how best to contribute to climate change mitigation within the reach and limits of common but differentiated responsibilities and respective capabilities.

Doha Climate Conference (COP18/CMP8).

Australia, EU, Japan, Lichtenstein, Monaco, Switzerland not carrying over any surplus trading credits (Assigned amounts) into the second commitment period of Kyoto Protocol, bears many positives, though I will argue that it was only the just and right step to take.

The positive being that this will reduce the strain on the Emissions Trading Systems (ETS) with already so many credits on the market which brought down the price and questioned the effectiveness of the ETS. With the Australian ETS – European Union ETS merger this year, amidst discussions to merge with the Swiss

ETS, it's obvious that countries committed to the ETS acted to strengthen the system. One could argue though that this was only fair given that the so-called assigned amounts surplus was not entirely generated through efficiency or technology interventions but rather because of the economic crisis which contracted production and national emissions.

A sound Emissions trading system (ETS) requires ambitious emissions targets and therefore it comes as no surprise that as a reward of sorts, "access to the Clean Development Mechanisms will be uninterrupted for all developed countries that have accepted targets for the second commitment period."

The Kyoto Protocol, as the only existing and binding agreement under which developed countries commit to cutting greenhouse gases, was amended so that it would continue.

Governments decided that the length of the second commitment period would be 8 years

The legal requirements that were to allow a smooth continuation of the Protocol were agreed upon.

The valuable accounting rules of the protocol were preserved. Countries that took on further commitments under the Kyoto Protocol agreed to review their emissions reduction commitments at the latest by 2014, with a view to increasing their respective levels of ambition.

The Kyoto Protocol's Market Mechanisms—the Clean Development Mechanisms (CDM), Joint Implementation (JI) and International Emissions Trading (IET) could continue.

Access to the mechanisms would be uninterrupted for all developed countries that accepted targets for the second commitment period.

JI would continue to operate, with the agreed technical rules allowing the issuance of credits once a host country's emissions target had been formally established.

Australia, the EU, Japan, Lichtenstein, Monaco and Switzerland declared that they would not carry over any surplus emissions trading credits (Assigned Amounts) into the second commitment period of the Kyoto Protocol.

New Market Mechanisms (NMM) were on the table for discussion, and seemingly satisfied the skeptics but the climate financing market harbours first mover advantages. Organisations interested in making climate change mitigations impact are better off piloting NMM such that they gather the needed knowledge for full scale implementation.

New Market Mechanisms

- A Work programme has been agreed to further elaborate the new market-based mechanism under the UNFCCC, and also sets out possible elements for its operation.
- A work programme to develop a framework for recognizing mechanisms established outside the UNFCCC, such as nationally-administered or bilateral offset programmes, and to consider their role in helping countries to meet their mitigation targets, has also been agree.

Discussing the effectiveness and environmental integrity of Carbon Capture & Storage projects under the Kyoto Protocol's Clean Development Mechanism is a welcome move because it is time we considered such carbon reductions for carbon credit purposes.

Carbon Capture and Storage

- Government meeting in Doha have looked at ways to ensure the effectiveness and environmental integrity of projects under the Kyoto Protocol's Clean Development Mechanisms that capture and store carbon emissions

Development and transfer of technology

- Countries have taken forward work on enabling the development and transfer of technologies that can help developing countries adapt and curb their emissions.

Story: How Climate Diplomacy is hurting Small Island Developing States

Two things are wrong with this title. One, climate diplomacy is supposed to be a good thing since it involves efforts by various nations to seek a common ground on climate intervention. It is supposed to be a good thing, but for statistical reasons it is not. If results from climate change negotiations were a number, they would be the 'Mean' or 'Average'. We know by now that the average is only the mean score, or in the terms of climate diplomacy – 'consensus'. The average does not reveal to us the variance and disparity that is swallowed up in its score. For countries or coalitions that are left out in the consensus by low negotiation, or financial muscle, Climate Diplomacy with all good aims and intentions, winds up harming them.

Secondly, it is not only Small Island Developing States (SIDS) that are affected by climate change, we all are. Hence the statement 'hurting SIDS' is null. But not quite. Although we are all affected, we are affected at different degrees. Most prone states and cities are increasingly bearing the full throttle of climate change, more than others. Dhaka, Manila, Bangkok, Yangon, Djakarta, Ho Chi Minh, and Kolkata are said to be at extreme risk of climate change effects. If we are frogs in boiling water, then Small Island states *seem* to be getting most of the heat. I use the word 'seem' because if the world doesn't act, we'll soon all be affected. As a result, when it comes to action to fight climate change, our average (consensus) ambitions to combat climate change (like targeting temperature to below 2degrees Centigrade) are inadequate for the integrity and survival of SIDS.

On reading the submissions of views put forward by coalitions, and nations Conference of the Parties (COP19/CMP9) on 11 – 12 November 2013 (Warsaw, Poland), one cannot help but observe the disparity in tone and urgency of the submission from the: Republic of Vanuatu; Lithuania and European Union; Coalition for Rainforest Nations (Bangladesh, Belize, Chad, Cote d'Ivoire, Democratic Republic of Congo, Dominica, Dominican Republic, Fiji, Gabon, Guyana, Honduras, Kenya, Liberia, Nigeria, Panama, Papua New Guinea, Republic of Congo, Sierra Leone, Uganda); and Brazil.

The Republic of Vanuatu makes it known that the most vulnerable region of the Small Island Developing States (SIDS) are threatened in their integrity and survival as nations due to the negative impacts of climate change. In paragraph 3 of their Submission, it is mentioned that

> *"Noticing the unsatisfactory level of fulfillment of the financial pledges and considering the fast pace of climate change induced impacts in the SIDS, the Republic of Vanuatu urges contributing Parties to timely fulfill their pledges."*

In the submission by Lithuania, and the EU (supported by Albania, Bosnia and Herzegovina, the Former Yugoslav Republic of Macedonia, Montenegro, and Serbia.) the urgency voiced by SIDS is clearly missing. Regarding the Conventions Financial Mechanism of Green Climate Fund the EU's submission reads,

> *"It is the view of the EU that we should await this report, and particularly on the results of the ongoing efforts to develop the business model of the GCF, before deciding on guidance to the fund."*

My country Uganda, our neighbors—Democratic Republic of Congo, Kenya, and other sixteen countries under the Coalition for

Rainforest Nations, focus their submission on the functioning of the financial mechanisms (FM) with clear disagreement with the EU on the efficiency of the mechanisms in place. Short of stressing the time factor leaves SIDS vulnerable and isolated in the climate negotiations.

While the European Union and their partners explain that, the

> *"Global Environment Facility (GEF) support at the country level is well aligned with national priorities, shows progress toward impact at the local level, and enables countries to meet their obligations to the Conventions",*

the Coalition for Rainforest Nations disagrees, submitting instead for

> *"Conference of the Parties to improve coherence and coordination in the delivery of financial and technical support for implementation."*

Noting a *'mitigation ambition gap'*, the coalition calls for expanding market-based mechanisms and new funds to deliver new and additional public finance to fight climate change in the short and long term.

What should the world look out for at the climate conferences? Certainly, the state of the environment requires more ambitions in responding to climate change in addition to efforts of putting into action existing promises such as the Green Climate Fund (GCF) and streamlining the Global Environment Facility (GEF). In those two days, Small Island Developing States (SIDS) experiencing sea level rise require speed actionable commitments and additional funds to remedy the impact already being experienced.

When asked for his order, my friend has a way of getting the best gelato, he simply says "Surprise me!". Many people, young and old, will be hoping future COP/CMP convenings to surprise us—positively in the interest of the environment.

Compromises will have to be made. If future generations were to attend COP conferences, there are some things too important and urgent they would not compromise on. But they will not attend. Granted I ask but one favor, that an empty seat be reserved for their memory. That as decisions are being made, negotiators saliently consider the toll climate change has on their survival, and dignity.

CLIMATE INACTION

Externalities

L isette is very passionate about the environment, poverty eradication and sustainable development in general. She loves cycling, which is kind of cliché for the Dutch, playing tennis and being in touch with nature. Africa is her second home, though at times it seems her preferred settlement, at least that's what I thought when we last met in Utrecht, that despite the happy bars, beautiful canals and bridges nostalgia for East Africa was ever present but unspoken.

On the famed Dutch relationship with cycling, the 1973 Middle East oil crisis coupled with a rise in the number of deaths by motor vehicles persuaded the Dutch government to invest in improved cycling infrastructure. Anna Holligan in her BBC piece *'Why is cycling so popular in the Netherlands?'* identified how these two externalities were a huge driving force for the Dutch embracing a cycling culture when oil-producing countries stopped exports to the US and Western Europe. Anna writes that

> *'The jump in car numbers caused a huge rise in the number of deaths on Dutch roads with more than 3,000 people killed by motor vehicles, 450 of them children in 1971.'*

Guess who 'killed' the Horse-Drawn Carriage? No, it wasn't the invention of steam engine technology, nor was it the train; it was the accumulation of horse waste/manure in the streets which reached a tipping point in the cognitive tolerance levels of residents. The animal waste leeching into waterways, creating health and sanitation problems, which acted as a timely externality aided the car and train to cease to be a fiery tale but rather to be perceived as a savior from the plague of street horse waste.

An additional externality was the fact that increasingly more people started to traverse long distances regularly, rendering walking, and horse-drawn carriages impracticable.

Dror Etzion and Jeroen Struben (McGill University, Canada) provide an interesting analysis on the disruptive force of externalities in the automobile industry in their Oikos case study *"Better Place: Shifting Paradigms in the Automotive Industry"*.

Climate change externalities already exist, long and severely cold winters resulted in many deaths not to mention high gas utility bills. With severe summers, air conditioning bills are also poised to skyrocket with many people especially the elderly and young at high risk of death.

The April 2013 floods in central Europe damaged a lot of property and infrastructure, with the economic loss in Germany alone estimated as high as 12 billion Euros ($15.4 billion).

We claim to be an adaptive society, innovative generation yet tend to rely on externalities to shift our consumption and behavioral patterns.

Elting Morison in *'Gunfire at Sea: A Case Study of Innovation'* explains that

> *"We are not yet emotionally an adaptive society, though we try systematically to develop forces that tend to make us one, we encourage the search for new inventions; we keep the mind stimulated, bright and free to seek out fresh means of communication, energy; yet we remain in part, appalled by the consequence of our ingenuity, and too frequently try to find security, through the shoring up to ancient conventions, the extension of purely physical safeguards"*

We are frogs in boiling water that need to be taken out and thrown back to realize that the temperature is not the same as ere, that all along the water has been heating up, but more than ever we need to be reminded that we are not the best friends of change when we need it the most. Perhaps the expectations that we have accumulated on how adaptive and innovative we are is at best an attempt to cover-up our dependence on externalities to shift us to where we dream but do not dare to travel. It is a journey.

Climate Change Debates

I theorize that the continued focus on the climate change debate has deprived us the opportunity to focus on the climate itself, and how best we could mitigate, adapt or even better our interaction with the environment.

But there is a second theory. We are exactly were climate change deniers want us to be. Keeping the debate on climate change causation is one way of avoiding discussing or acting on the evident impacts of global climate change. In fact Brenda Ekwurzel, in her article 'Climate Disinformation Continues to Harm U.S. Communities' makes the point that Climate Disinformation uses an old playbook of

> *'when scientists discover that your products are risky, attack the science.'*

Besides keeping the debate on climate change itself and attacking the scientific bases, climate deniers do employ other more subtle tactics. One such strategy is to isolate climate change from environment and sustainability discussions. It is not appealing to ignore the human effects of deforestation, water pollution, resource waste fueling climate change. Climate change deniers are aware that the smog and poor air quality plaguing industrialized cities like Beijing, and Mexico are a no-go area. They are also aware that famine, drought, floods emanating from human activity are self-evident impacts of human induced climate change.

The ambiguity surrounding sustainability, a concept open to various meanings and interpretations plays well into the hands of climate change deniers, another motivation for developing a comprehensive definition further. In fact, it not be nice if in the next conference of parties meeting this fall, negotiators work around establishing a robust actionable definition?

Climate Change deniers have an unlikely friend in individuals who are looking forward to gigantic environmental catastrophes as a prelude to an Armageddon like judgement of earth's inhabitants. As they hope to be 'raptured' aware, climate change is no big deal for them since they do not expect to be around to experience the extremities of climatic breakdown. But there is a folly in this belief, as God placed man and woman onto this earth to cultivate and care for it. This theme resonates in the Book of Genesis found in the Bible. In Pope Francis World Environment Day Speech which appearing in Huffington post of Jun 05, 2013, he says

> 'When we talk about the environment, my thoughts turn to the Book of Genesis, which states that God placed man and woman on earth to cultivate and care for it.'

Someone else is talking to us, and that is the environment itself. According to Pratma Bansal and Kendall Roth, the environment itself has the potential of driving ecological considerations. This is in their article 'Why Companies Go Green: A methodology of ecological responsiveness', wherein the authors explore how the natural environment itself can cause companies to go green as one of many stakeholders. In this regard, the ferociously changing environment will increasingly make the point of an ecosystem strained beyond her carrying capacity.

A Paradigm Shift. The change process needed to reduce emissions and natural ecosystem resource depletion needs to be oiled to shift from a reactive approach of mitigation to a proactive approach of improving the ecosystem. Change itself is the culprit. A change that is neither slow nor slight.

In Elting Morison's article *"Gunfire at Sea: A case study of Innovation"* the author makes the point that

> *'the tendency is apparently involuntary and immediate to protect oneself against the shock of change by continuing in the presence of altered situations the familiar habits however incongruous of the past.'*

Change is difficult both from an individual point of view and also from an organization point of view, Reasons for Inertia are: Learning new ways and having to unlearn the old; Costs involved in the change process (though I have on several occasions explained that these so called costs are vague); and Cognition thus we need to be careful about our strengths because these could create inertia to embrace change to a more sustainable way of doing business.

Path dependence explains that our decisions for a given circumstances might be limited by the decisions we have made in the past, even though the circumstances under which those decisions were made in the past changed. This is what Elting Morison's calls *'continuing in the presence of altered situations the familiar habits'*. Finding the right answers to sustainable growth will depend on the extent to which we dwell on our past experiences as a standard. We must remember that standards that are first-to-market can become entrenched (like the QWERTY layout in typewriters still being used in computer keyboards).

Inferior standards can persist simply because of the legacy they have built up presents a sustainability challenge since as previously mentioned, sustainability requires change.

How do we shape the climate change discourse? We need to start by identifying the points of friction or tension in the social economic structure which are produced by climate change adaptation/mitigation or environmental betterment. We also need to ask ourselves why those points of friction are produced, and perhaps more importantly, what, if anything may be done about them.

Why should you care? I have read the closing chapter of this climate change stalemate and neither greens not climate change deniers win in the end. We are all already losing due to the economic and human loss arising from consistent neglect and procrastination in tackling climate change. We could turn this whole thing around by perceiving the chaotic climate as a wakeup call to do something, just like H.G. Wells said,

> 'Affliction comes to us, not to make us sad but sober; not to make us sorry but wise.'

If we claim to love our shared home, then we should embrace Erich Segal's concept of love, for

> 'Love means not ever having to say you're sorry'.

Debate is healthy because it helps bring understanding to communities. However, the playing field is far from even. For example, whilst we climate change mitigation enthusiasts are working within the strict limitations of scientific research, change skeptics seldom perpetrate myths. One such myth is that the efforts by households to convert waste into clean cooking charcoal to reduce the cutting of trees is somehow connected to a plan of creating a green leftist world government.

Another myth is that global warming has been on a hiatus. Andrew Glikson, an Earth, and Paleo-climate scientist at the Australian National University today wrote a brilliant piece dispelling these myths – scientifically.

I hope the climate change debate eventually shifts from *'is climate change happening?'* to a more progressive *'what can we do about it?'* In his piece *'IPCC climate trends: Blueprints for tipping points'* is written for the Business Spectator. He closes perfectly, *'Good planets are hard to come by.'*

Climate Talks

'Full moon is falling through the sky. Cranes fly through clouds. Wolves howl. I cannot find rest Because I am powerless To amend a broken world.'

— GUY GAVRIEL KAY, UNDER HEAVEN

The UN Framework Convention on Climate Change, G-8, the Major Economies Forum, and the UN Secretary General are on a global scale attempting to reach an agreeable comprehensive climate treaty to address the threat that Climate Change is.

Although the negotiations appear polarized between the most-at-risk Vs the least-at-risk, another obstacle is regarding interpretation of the meaning of the Principal of Common but Differentiated Responsibilities and Respective Capabilities (CBDRRC). At the center of this impasse is the question of

'Who Pays for climate change response?'

Lesser developed countries that have historically emitted less, argue that they have fewer responsibilities from this historical perspective. Also taking into account respective capabilities, one could argue further that irrespective of historical emissions, these nations are resourcefully less capable of responding to climate change They also argue that by virtue of their status as developing countries, have fewer resources to devote to climate change mitigation or adaptation. They therefore wish for this principal to be binding in this regard.

This seems to ignore observations of rampant environmental degradations that also least developed countries are subjecting to their ecosystems. There is a risk that if only rich nations issue finance fostering of adaptive societies to curtail climate change, the underlying causes and consequences of environmental degradation may persist.

A few developed countries, most notably the US have a different take on CBDRRC arguing instead that this being a 'Principle' should have minimal or no binding power as law. None of these positions seems to reflect the reality of current development trends in which the developing countries are growing at some of the highest GDP rates and will soon migrate into the haves. Already countries like China, South Africa, Angola, Cape Verde, are making significant economic strides and if the burden of financing climate change responses is left to the narrow definition of developed, emerging, and developing, then we are missing the point.

Some developed countries are yet to show leadership in championing climate change response domestically, how then can they be entrusted with the global response? In any case, waiting for the global movement to catch steam in solving this challenge might take long – as already has. Although countries that have historically polluted more should contribute to the solution commensurately, we might recall that poor countries are growing fast and contributing to environmental destruction. Not all counties are signatories of these treaties or party to the Kyoto Protocol. Hence the need for alternative approaches to respond to climate change concurrently as we continue to pursue a global agreement.

> 'It does not take a great supernatural heroine or magical hero to save the world. We all save it every day, and we all destroy it — in our own small ways — by every choice we make and every tiniest action resulting from that choice'

– VERA NAZARIAN.

We could start with education, not only to reduce the misinformation on climate change, alter our consumption patterns through the power of our purchases. In buying products that are good for the environment we create a powerful chain of events that attract dollars to green investment and sustainable business. But these efforts can be in vain as unscrupulous businesses can willfully falsify product brand and package as green to capture market. Sound regulatory framework and suitable testing technologies could be used to abet such unscrupulous practices. Then we need to galvanize the process by electing leaders with the courage to embed sustainability in all government programs and provide the appropriate regulatory environment to foster green economy to thrives.

Investing in environmentally conscious solutions is good for economic reasons too. The costs associated with addressing climate change fade in comparison to the cost of financing reconstruction efforts after climatic disasters. It is cheaper to reduce emissions today and curb environmental degradation than to wait to rebuild, not to mention the human toll such disasters leave in their wake.

Climate & development -
Perceived tradeoffs

Some argue that

> *poor countries should be allowed to pollute as much as they*
> *want because the developed world had to first pollute dur-*
> *ing the industrial age to reach developed status.*

'Greening Industrialization' offers more benefits. For instance, human capital is a hugely significant pillar for any society's growth and as such ensuring healthy living through abating pollution, and climate change mitigation/adaptation are all beneficial to any nation, poor or not. Can also be said that investments in healthy environments saves the healthcare costs that go in treating the environmental degradation impacts.

Unabated environmental degradation as a price for development omits one important fact. Most developing nations are highly dependent on agricultural production with more than half of their populations employed in agricultural sector. It is no secret that developing nations are the food basket of the world, from which vital revenue is obtained. This creates an extra impetus for promoting green industry by encouraging efficient resource use and reduction in pollution to facilitate a development whose growth does not necessarily result in rampant pollution or excessive resource extraction.

The question of whether developing countries can afford not to pollute ought to be asked differently; instead, we should ask can developing countries afford the consequences of pollution and eco-degradation. Clearly not, because most developing countries have the least preparation and technical sophistication to absorb the destruction from climate extremities and all hazards that come from unsustainable practice. Climate change negotiations and treaties need to be re-imagined by looking at the environment as the main customer and not merely a party. In the eyes of the environment, there are no poor nations or rich nations; there are just acts of degradations. It is insignificant whether that degradation comes from a chimney in China, USA, or Europe, or if the degradation comes from the unsustainable felling of trees for charcoal, farming, settlement etc. We are all responsible, and as such have a common obligation. There is no harm in wealthier nations supporting other countries to stabilize the global ecosystem if the recipients contribute to reducing their own environmental footprint.

Demystifying the slow response to Climate Change.

I suppose the question some would ask is

> why the deafening silence about climate change? When the impact of climate change seems obvious, why then is the green economy discussion still polarized to its extremes?

Perhaps by exploring various dimensions of sustainability, we might be able to have a knowledgeable discussion and understand each other better. I proceed int he next paragraphs to explain these facets further.

Shareholder Engagement Vs Stakeholders Engagement.
Who bears residual risk? Shareholders are often perceived as being sole bearers of residual risk, and thus management's role being to function as stewards of shareholder's wealth to align control with residual risk. If the residual risk fully rests with the shareholders and yet the control lies with management, this mismatch of residual risk and control ought to be reconciled through shareholder

engagement to make sure the company grows in the direction that the shareholders so desire.

However, other stakeholders do experience hazards, and risks, resulting from the operation of firms. Therefore, shareholders are not the only bearers of residual risk, because employees, society, government, customers, flora, and fauna etc. can all bear residual risk. Thus, shareholder engagement is a misalignment. To properly align all residual risk with control we need to engage all stakeholders, a shift from Shareholder engagement to Stakeholder engagement.

Tragedy of commons (Prisoner's Dilemma)

The tragedy of the commons in refers to condition in which we each try to maximize fulfilment of our individual needs irrespective of others, resulting in overuse and depletion of the commonly held resource. For example, if I own a small piece of land on which to graze a maximum of 40 cattle, I will naturally not graze over 40 cattle. However, if the land is public, you might find more than 50 cattle grazing. It could begin with one farmer reasoning that a small addition to the total stock will contribute little harm to the available pasture. However, if other farmers reason likewise, these incremental additions to the stock using the land lead to overgrazing and thus the destruction of the resource itself.

Sustainability is aimed at avoiding the problem of commons because if each individual in this situation rationally pursues his or her own short-term interest while disregarding others similarly pursuing theirs, then the long-run consequence is that everyone loses their share in the collective resource.

Altruism Vs Egoism

Altruism enthusiasts argue that moral decisions should be based upon the interests or well-being of others rather than on self-interest. On the other hand, egoism is belief that one ought to do what is in one's own self-interest.

Sustainability is an altruistic moral choice, to take on the moral obligation to help or serve others, or the greater good of life. This is one way of addressing the problem of commons. However, it is only fair to mention that some people reason that we all generally act out of self-interest, which therefore means that altruism – in its pure form does not exists, thus altruism=egoism. In this case only regulation can adequately intervene to avert climate change since when left on our own we are incapable of acting altruistically.

Path Dependence & QWERTY

Path dependence explains that our decisions for a given circumstances might be limited by the decisions we have made in the past, even though the circumstances under which those decisions were made in the past have changed.

This raises a serious question for Sustainability and how we solve problems about sustainability. Finding the right answers to sustainable growth will depend on the extent to which we dwell on our past experiences as a standard. We must remember that standards that are first-to-market can become entrenched (like the QWERTY layout in typewriters still being used in computer keyboards).

Inferior standards can persist simply because of the legacy they have built up which presents a sustainability challenge since as previously mentioned, sustainability might require change.

Change is difficult both from an individual point of view, and from an organizational point of view. Reasons for Inertia are: Learning new ways and having to unlearn the old; Cost involved in the change process; Cognition, thus companies need to be careful about their strengths because these could create inertia to embrace change to a more sustainable way of doing business.

Theory of conformism & Agentic State (Obedience to Authority)

The challenge posed by individuals trying to conform to groups of reference is that if someone has neither the ability nor the expertise to make decisions, especially in a crisis, they will leave decision making to the group and its hierarchy. The group is the person's behavioral model. To effectively address the sustainability challenge, we need to recognize that it is not just individual behavior and decisions we are dealing with, but also group actions & decisions.

The agentic state theory observes that a person comes to view themselves as the instrument for carrying out another person's wishes, and they therefore no longer see themselves as responsible for their actions. Once this critical shift of viewpoint has occurred in the person, all the essential features of obedience follow. Therefore, individuals are not likely to consider sustainability issues if they perceive their actions as those of another. Thus, little or no gilt since they are merely only acting as agents.

Invention as mother of necessity Vs Necessity as mother of invention.

Invention as mother of necessity follows the thought that we create useful innovations/inventions that we gradually become dependent upon and consequently create a need. While necessity as mother of invention ascribes to the thought that we face problems first and, in our response, we seek to find solutions to fix those problems, thus invention.

When we approach sustainability, we need both mindsets, because sustainability could require us to solve problems before they happen, anticipate challenges, and solve them in time. In other words, we do not have to fall in the gutter to know that it will get us dirty -thus invention as mother of necessity.

However, we also need to be able to solve problems that occur in the present considering necessity as mother of invention.

The problem of problem choice.

Sustainability is about recognizing that we not only have a problem, but also a problem of problem choice. For example, if we go the direction of stakeholder engagement, who are our stakeholders? Should we say considering our customers, society, government is sufficient? Which problems of our stakeholders should we address? How far do we go?

Sustainability truly involves addressing the problem of problem choice.

Regulation.

It is important to ensure that we not only make regulation but look at how effective the regulation can be in terms of driving behavior. Companies driven by the bottom line will tend to evaluate the likelihood of being caught and if caught, the penalty vis-à-vis the opportunity of breach. Therefore, it is not sufficient to make regulation, but rather to evaluate the regulations and find out if the expected behavior was achieved.

Imperfections of Market system.

Markets are imperfect as they are characterized by haggling, contracts, regulation; transaction costs, all of which ought to be factored into as we address sustainability challenges.

Boiling frogs or frogs in boiling water?

Are we frogs thrown in hot boiling water or are we frogs boiling in water? This too is a sustainability challenge. We are likely to observe the changes in our society and environment that need fixing if we are looking outward from a freshly new mindset and thus are frogs thrown in boiling water. Woe unto us if we are using a historical frame of thinking to solve present and future problems for, we stand the risk of not realizing the rising water temperature and turn into boiling frogs.

Sustainability as a journey, and the grey areas.

Sustainability is a journey, and for a while there was a bit of a contradiction when I encountered the Corporate Citizenship model that suggested a stage by stage process, with a beginning and a peak. Some firms perceive Sustainability through three business lenses: One of pure business-as-usual; the second as bolt-on sustainability; and finally, one of embedded sustainability.

My interpretation is that various schools of thought are trying to make the sustainability concept understandable by creating a stage by stage process. On analyzing the companies, there was a mismatch in terms of the fact that, they are neither here nor there, even within the same company you find business units at various stages of sustainability, and this distinction is greater when geographical comparisons come to play.

These occurrences are a confirmation and not a contradiction to the fact that sustainability is indeed a journey at individual, firm, and government level. Also, this is an early sign to exercise a lot of caution and listening to be aware of the grey areas and avoid jumping to conclusions too early.

Thoughts on the struggles of the Electric Car.

For over 100 years, the Electric car has been tried at various times by various people/companies. These efforts have significantly quickened the possibility of ultimately having a dominant technology, through the reduction of barriers and misconceptions surrounding this industry.

The role of a standard. There is need for a universally enforceable standard on the batteries, charging systems, and various other peripherals to reduce switching costs for customers and increase user accessibility of compatible processes or parts. The challenge is that, only a few of the required standards are in place notwithstanding the challenge of enforceability with governments seeming reluctant to move in this direction. Regulation is very important, if not the most important driver.

Cut-throat competition in the motor industry. The key companies in Detroit, Japan, Germany are singly developing their ideas to try to create a dominant innovation. This is positive and negative at the same time. Positive because it means the emerging innovation will probably capture the market, negative in the sense that every manufacturer wants their innovation to be the standard, to gain advantage. Thus, delaying the transformation to electric.

Stretch of sight. A risk for short term perspectives with immediate sales volumes today, jeopardizing thought about possible future opportunities. Corporations today are not well placed to innovate and invent such disruptive technologies for two reasons; the *new Electric vehicles could cannibalize the existing brands based on Internal combustion*; and secondly, companies and CEO performance is largely tied to how the stock index performs as a result of sales and margin, therefore few CEO are confident or willing to take the risk of push the idea in the board rooms.

Capturing Value, Environment, & External Forces. The innovator/ inventor is not usually the one who captures value but the one in the *chain towards the dominant strategy*. Convenience, Cost, and performance are key to any technology. These have been inhibiting mass adoption of this technology. People are not usually willing to compromise convenience nor performance, even in the face of environmental hazards.

External forces have a huge impact in the adoption of technology, but those external forces must be significant to cause any realistic changes in consumer behavior. Previous transportation technologies destroyed the inertial to change with help of external forces. Unfortunately, Electric cars do not have a similar equivalent externality, yet. Diesel needed the fuel scarcity; the horse carriage needed the increased waste in the street to cause change to petrol.

So far, environmental concern has proven not strong enough to cause a significant shift in consumption.

To truly create and capture value, Electric Cars need to position as convenient, cost friendly, and performing whilst simultaneously promoting a standard.

Human contribution to climate change

Earth has a lot of time in the universe, we do not.

The Intergovernmental Panel on Climate Change (IPCC) concluded in the Fifth Assessment Report (WGI AR5) that with 95% certainty, humans are to blame for climate change.

If a doctor had told an at-risk client that they were 95% certain of imminent health complications unless certain changes are made, most people who act immediate to avert the danger. *Why isn't that the case when it comes to combating climate change?* In the headline statements from the summary for policymakers, it is noted that

'Human influence on the climate system is clear'

The IPCC also states that

"The rate of sea level rise since the mid-19th century has been larger than the mean rate during the previous two millennia"

To avert the looming and existing risks, we will have to change, to cleaner sources of energy, reduce pollution; efficiently manage the value chain of processes that support our fragile existence.

Knowingly or unknowingly, Change-phobia will instinctively start to search for mistakes in the IPCC report. People will eagerly be looking for follies in the science to act as anesthetics to numb the seriousness of the state of our climate. However willful blindness is perilously a temporary sedative, because after the scientists, the weather starts to speak, and if the events of this year are anything to go by, when the weather speaks, the price is enormous.

We can do something. We can teach our children, family, and friends to make informed choices in their living patterns. We can also vote with our purchases, by buying products that are neutral or better still, good for the environment. Then we can vote in leaders who recognize and are committed to bettering life after tomorrow. We are already living in the life after tomorrow. What used to appear as a sustainability cause for future generations is now today's reality. The floods, fires, landslides, climate migration, escalation of disease, have all consumed our headlines these past months. Climate change is here, and it is us who stand to gain from action or suffer from inaction/procrastination.

Many times, we may have noticed but willfully kept a blind eye, perhaps because mitigating climate change appears to interfere with our way of life. However, this is a self-defeating stance, an oxymoron. If we really cared about having a good time, then we would embrace efforts to combat climate change to ensure that the happiness we pursue lasts longer and is not merely a comet appearance.

Is it too late to stop climate change? This question appears to refer to our lifetimes, or generation. And therefore, the implication of the question is whether it is possible to stop climate change for our good, and in our lifetime. While the substance of sustainability is to look beyond the present, this is a vital question if human lives will be saved soon. In fact, one could argue that even future generation are a function of present generations, and thus ensuring the survival or betterment of the present generations is implicitly beneficial to future existence.

At the end of the question *'is it too late to stop climate change?'* I would add, *'for whom?'* That is, late for us, or for future generations? Climatic changes take long periods of time, and the recent extremes in weather events are a result of previous acts of environmental degradation. Similarly, and unfortunately so, today's acts of pollution, and inefficient resource extraction will affect future generations in form of ill health, extreme weather events, all amidst resource scarcity.

Anthropogenic effects on the environment might appear slow but cumulatively have very dire consequences on the environment. For example, ozone in the earth's atmosphere declines at a rate of about 4% per decade; a single chlorine atom is known to keep on destroying ozone for up to two years; between 1751 and 1994 surface ocean pH is estimated to have decreased from approximately 8.25 to 8.14, representing an increase of almost 30% in acidity in the world's oceans with negative consequences for oceanic calcifying organisms.

For many people in Sardinia (Italy), like Philippines recently, and earlier Solomon Islands, Australia, China, Central Europe, Peru, USA, Mexico, Somalia, Mozambique, Kenya, Uganda, Turkey, Sahel region, Indonesia, Malaysia, Ecuador, Wales (UK)…climate change mitigation efforts came too late. They have already experienced the toll record breaking weather extremities.

The loss of life and property experienced thus far makes one to wonder where the climate change mitigation efforts which came too late for many, are already late for at least the next 'few' years in which we will continue to experience dramatic weather effects of colossal damage.

Where does that leave you and me? Adaptation. We need to incorporate in our infrastructure, building designs the aspect of adapting to climate change to reduce the damage emanating from human induced climate change as and when it occurs.

We are not late to stop the incidence and severity of climate change, more especially for future generation. For them, we can make efforts for climate change mitigation. We can, but will we?

Story - Rosia Montana: When your neighbor's house is on fire, carry water.

Despite several years passing since protestors in 2013 successfully halted expansion of mining activity at Romania's picturesque Rosia Montana, the town is still on edge, not knowing whether the government will reintroduce plans to set up the gold mine. This community is longing for certainty to be able to move on with their lives normally.

One winter's day, with spring fast approaching, I hurriedly walked from a Brussels' metro stop to escape another of Belgium's cold but beautiful nights. What I did not expect was to stumble upon an almost identical setup as that in Gyula Halasz classical picture taken in the collection 'Parris de Nuit' (Paris at Night). I picked the camera and captured my rare find (above right) in honor of a photographer whom I reverently admire and respect. Many things are missing in this picture, the bright car lights, the wet rainy environment, the lamps were a little higher... more importantly it lacks the Gyula Halasz touch. It is said that at a time when pictures were not considered respectable art, Gyula, having not found much success in painting chose to use the pseudonym 'Brassia', Hungarian for the city of Brasov, situated in

Romania. Also beautiful like Brassia's pictures; Romania herself! Romania is blessed with nature still drawing her own designs and patterns in the mountains and valleys, with flora blossoming in season. An ever-looming mining project now threatens to spoil the Rosia Montana peaks involving the use of toxic cyanide wreaking havoc in a very picturesque area let alone contaminate ground water with cyanide.

Despite the low media coverage which left Romanians in their almost solitary struggle, the streets of Bucharest were filled with people on Monday 9th September 2013, all hoping for a green future and safe environment for their nation. Their courage, resilience and unity have not wavered, and eventually paid off as the mining plans were abandoned, for now at least. When your neighbor's house is on fire, it is wise to carry plenty of water, not only for his/her house, but also for your own. Today is Romania's test, no one knows whose challenge it will be tomorrow. The Rosia Montana community is longing for certainty that this is not another on and off again prospect to be able to live normally and invest comfortably in the village.

GREEN ENERGY
& SDGS

Achieving the Sustainable development Goals (SDGs) and helping raise those at the Bottom of the Pyramid (BoP) are increasingly being supported by innovative solar powered applications. This should not come as a surprise since access to energy goes to the very heart of livelihoods. According to the International Energy Agency (IEA) 1.4 Billion people do not have access to electricity, nearly a quarter of the world's population.

Most people would associate solar with household lighting; fewer would associate solar with refrigeration, mobile phone charging, solar lanterns, internet, and learning centers.

Innovations around solar have gone beyond these applications to include solar water pumps, pay-as-you-go solar solutions, solar streetlights, and various lifesaving plug and play solar products.

Plug and Play Solar Products.
Solar Suitcase (by We Care Solar). The Solar Suitcase provides health workers with medical lighting and power for mobile communication, computers, and medical devices. It is therefore suitable for a range of medical and humanitarian settings. Equipping off-grid medical clinics with solar power for medical and surgical lighting, facilitates emergency care, reducing maternal and infant morbidity and mortality.

Sustainable Development Goal (SDG) 3 (*By 2030 reduce the global maternal mortality ratio to less than 70 per 100,000 live births*) can be achieved if healthcare is extended to off-grid rural areas using such innovative technology.

Solar Ear. Solar Ear Brazil, manufactures, assembles, and distributes digital rechargeable hearing aid, a new solar battery charger and rechargeable hearing aid batteries which costs the same as disposable zinc air batteries, but lasts 2 to 3 years. Solar Ear resulted from a partnership of Brazilian Foundation, Instituto CEFAC, social marketing organization Legar, plus several University stakeholders and in conjunction with the youths who are deaf, from an NGO in Africa.

Sustainable Development Goal (SDG) 4 target 4.1 states that by *2030, ensure that all girls and boys complete free, equitable and quality primary and secondary education.* However, disability is keeping otherwise healthy children and adults from going to school and working as they are considered deaf. Those affected suffer from the lack of educational and occupational opportunities. This takes us back to SDG1 target 1.1 (By 2030 eradicate extreme poverty for all people everywhere, currently measured as people living on less than $1.25 a day) because without educational and occupational opportunities poverty can increase.

Solar Powered Internet and learning centers

As a United Nations special report notes, Internet access has become

> *"an indispensable tool for realizing a range of human rights, combating inequality, and accelerating development and human progress."*

Citing the critical role that the Internet has played in the protection and promotion of basic human rights.

Green-Wifi. Multiple solar-powered Wi-Fi hotspots were set up on the campus of EFACAP school in Lascahobas, Haiti. This initiative brought affordable, reliable, and sustainable broadband access to 6 regions and 20 un-served population centers across Haiti.

NICE concept. This is a business model to distribute development products and services in Bottom of the Pyramid (BoP) markets, through a network of solar-powered ICT centers operated by local entrepreneurs on a franchise-basis. The products and services offered in NICE Centers have the potential to help people in developing countries towards income generation. Currently NICE has seven operational centers in The Gambia, West Africa.

Solar Cubed. Stands for Energy. Education. Empowerment. They have a simple set-up, which is an all-in-one solution combining two 90W solar panels and a DC charge controller, that enable computing in off-grid and resource constrained locations. Due to the power-frugal laptops which are charged while they are simultaneously in use. By the time that the solar panels are no longer producing energy, the laptops are charged sufficiently to run for many more hours.

Solar LEAP. Both the monitors and computers are designed to run on 12V direct current power inputs, so they can be run directly off a solar-powered car battery or run on mains power using a standard 'brick' power adapter. In addition to the hardware, SolarLEAP preloads each computer with Ubuntu further lowering the cost. In Nepal and Ghana, 15 schools and one orphanage have been using these computers for over a year.

In terms of SDGs these projects are directly promoting income generation and learning, i.e. SDG 1 and 4. These projects also pass on the principles of sustainable development and relevance of environmental resources which also promotes attaining of SDG 13

These series of efforts in various remote parts of the world have potential to pick-up BoP communities. From the interventions shown above these projects have a resultant effect of addressing some of the SDGs.

Pay-As-You-Go Solar Solutions.

Despite living in the sunniest parts of the world or surrounding areas, a great number are still without access to the national electricity grid or any other form of clean energy source due to high upfront cost, Inflexible payment schemes, and not least high cost of loan collection for micro-finance institutions. Innovative solar products cost money, and when the intended beneficiaries are people at the bottom of the pyramid, it then requires even more innovative financing solutions. One such solution is the use of pay-as-you-go solar arrangement.

There are various eye-catching pay-as-you-go solar solutions, which if applied well might alleviate the burden of relatively high initial capital expenditure –in the context of rural subsistence-based communities.

Sonopro Power & Light, Inc, founded by John Steininger and Doug Vilsack, offers a product known as Divi Light which works on pre-paid enablement periods (EPs). Straight out of the box, a Divi light is enabled for 1 week. After that, enablement periods (EPs) must be transferred onto the lamp through it's built in short range wireless connection to re-enable operation. EPs can be purchased from Divi Dealers, from Divi Agents, and from other Divi lamp owners. A Divi Agent can transfer enabling periods (EPs) to your lamp from his/her prepaid account using a smart phone.

Anyone can become a Divi agent using either a Divi Light or a smart phone running their Divi app. Once the Divi Light has used enough EPs, the lamp is un-locked, forever. The lamp operates payment-free from then on. Lamp-to-lamp transfers work with all Divi lamps – locked or un-locked. The Divi Light concept started with a trial phase with over 100 customers in Southern Africa and went on to scaleup. I find this solution reflecting the day to day way of life in most African societies where it is common for neighbors to share resources. In this case neighbors can share and/or lend each other enabling periods (EPs).

Hessex, led by an Australian entrepreneur, Boyd Whalan, provides a solar lighting system solution allowing customers to buy solar lighting systems on a pay-as-you-use basis, using their mobile phones to purchase power. Once the sum of the repayments equals the total cost of the system is paid, the solar lighting is free to use for the lifetime of the system. This approach avoids the high upfront costs of retail solar lighting systems and ensures solar power is accessible to those with low, inconsistent incomes. Boyd has already built a prototype, having come up with the idea when he spent six weeks volunteering in Ghana with not-for-profit organization.

Simpa Networks, sells distributed energy solutions on a *'Progressive Purchase'* basis to underserved consumers in emerging markets. Customers make a small initial down payment for a solar PV system and then pre-pay for the energy service, topping up their systems in small user-defined increments using a mobile phone. Each payment for energy also adds towards the final purchase price. Once fully paid, the system unlocks permanently and produces energy, free. Simpa launched starting in Karnataka, India.

Azuri Technologies headquartered in Cambridge, UK combines mobile phone and solar technology to provide solar-as-a-service by which the user pays for the usage of the solar product by purchasing weekly scratch cards. The Indigo scratch card is validated using SMS from a mobile phone and the resulting one-off passcode entered into the Indigo unit which causes it to operate for a period (typically a week). Customers can charge their mobile phone and have 8 hours of clean lighting for two rooms. After customers have paid off the cost of their unit, they have the option to upgrade to a larger system and access more energy.

M-KOPA offers solar-powered lighting and mobile charging in Kenya, Uganda, and Tanzania on a pay-as-you-go basis, with payment via M-PESA (M-PESA is a mobile phone based money transfer system) They provide a d.light solar home system with 3 bright lights and mobile charging. Since 2010 M-KOPA has helped Kenyans acquire solar power products by offering innovative payment plans and a distribution model tailored to the needs of their customers. M-KOPA Solar is available through select M-KOPA dealers in Kenya, initially focused in Western Kenya. In 2020 M-KOPA reported having connected over 750,000 homes and business to affordable solar power.

Numerous other pay-as-you-go solar solutions like Solar Gem, Bright Solar Power, Angaza Design, Stima Systems, Off-Grid Electric, Lumos, Grundfos Lifelink are also available.

We have seen solutions in India, Kenya, South Africa anchoring on broadly accessible technology such as the mobile phone expansion in developing countries. We have also seen entrepreneurs from USA, Australia, United Kingdom, and Kenya. One wonders, given the role of the 'connectors' or 'aggregators' or 'entrepreneurs', how best can we facilitate these salient yet vital actors, to accelerate sustainability for all?

Fracking Conundrum

Clean Energy Vs Threat Of Earthquakes & Water-Soil Pollution.

To call fracking a conundrum, is still an understatement. We have to trade-off between having a clean source of energy, Shale gas, at a time when the energy demand is growing exponentially yet on the other hand lays the potential threat of rise in earthquakes & Water pollution resulting from fluids injected deep underground.

Hydraulic fracturing (fracking) is the process of drilling and injecting fluid into the ground at a high pressure in order to fracture shale rocks to release natural gas inside.

Energy security is another concern, more so at such a time when many governments cannot afford to continue to spend revenues importing natural gas from the regional monopolies. According to the International Energy Agency, the 27-member EU's dependence on gas imports will increase to 86 percent in 2035 from 61 percent in 2009, and the volume of imports will rise 74 percent. To further compound this puzzle, Gas is expected become a bigger part of energy mix, not least because of the severe and long winters emanating from climate change.

Bloomberg reported on April 12, 2012 (*Earthquake Outbreak in U.S. Tied to Fracking Wastewater*) that Researchers from the U.S. Geological Survey said that *for the three decades until 2000, seismic events in the nation's midsection averaged 21 a year. They jumped to 50 in 2009, 87 in 2010 and 134 in 2011.*

Huffington Posts reported on 08/07/2012 (*Fracking-Earthquake Connection Suggested In New Study*) that Earthquakes triggered by fluids injected deep underground, such as during the controversial practice of fracking, may be more common than previously thought.

State Impact in the article '*How Oil and Gas Disposal Wells Can Cause Earthquakes*' reported that the disposal of drilling wastewater used in fracking has now been scientifically linked to earthquakes. The fluids used in fracking (and the wastewater that comes back up the well) is disposed of by injecting it into disposal wells deep underground.

Yahoo News on October 2, 2012 (*Unusual Dallas Earthquakes Linked to Fracking, Expert Says*) reported that three unusual earthquakes that shook a suburb west of Dallas appear to be connected to the past disposal of wastewater from local hydraulic fracturing operations, according to a geophysicist who has studied earthquakes in the region.

Live Science on August 06, 2012 (*Fracking Earthquakes: Injection Practice Linked to Scores of Tremors*) reported a seismologist had identified th epicenters for 67 earthquakes — more than eight times as many as reported by the National Earthquake Information Centre — with magnitudes of 3.0 or less. Most were located within a few miles of one or more injection wells, suggesting injection-triggered quakes might be more common than thought.

France decided to keep Shale ban until a fracking alternative emerges. France's Industry Minister at the time, Arnaud Montebourg is quoted by Bloomberg saying, *"France isn't prepared to tap its shale energy resources until "clean technologies" are invented to replace hydraulic fracturing."*

In a Bloomberg report of May 23, 2012 (*European Fracking Bans Open Market for U.S. Gas Exports*) Bulgaria and France, home of the continent's largest estimated reserve, outlawed fracking over environmental concerns. Bulgaria banned hydraulic fracturing, and withdrew a license granted, after hundreds of *protesters marched in Sofia to oppose the technique, fearing it will pollute the water and soil in the nation's most fertile farm region of Dobrudja.*

Romania and Lithuania followed Ukraine in giving high-level backing to shale gas exploration, in a sign the political tide may be turning as central and eastern Europe looks to break free from reliance on Russian energy, according to a Financial Times report titled *Romania and Lithuania back fracking.*

CNN Business in May 3, 2013 article reported that UK ministers were consider offering communities fracking sweeteners with cheaper energy bills in exchange for dropping opposition to local fracking projects as part of plans to push ahead with shale-gas extraction.

South Africa – estimated to hold the world's fifth-largest reserves of shale gas – lifted a temporary halt on shale-gas exploration in an isolated, nature-rich region according to The Wall Street Journal of Sept. 7, 2012 (*South Africa Lifts Fracking Ban*). The country had imposed a moratorium on hydraulic fracturing—a procedure known as fracking—*while it took a closer look at the repercussions of letting companies use the controversial technique in the Karoo, an arid region home to a variety of desert mammals and plant species.* Strident opposition from environmental groups and the local community led to South Africa stopping exploration activity in the area. They fear that fracking, which involves blasting water mixed with sand and chemicals underground to free hydrocarbons trapped in rock, *could damage aquifers in the Karoo, harming the fragile ecosystem and threatening agriculture.*

What I find is that both sides of the fracking debate have their reasons. The defense for fracking points to the fact that the link between fracking and seismic activity is in specific areas where stressed faults already exist, and therefore fracking in other areas should not pose a huge threat. In which case, they point out that industry will self-regulate to avoid such locations or be supervised by the authorities. The challenge here is that, if the shale gas rich deposits are in areas already prone to seismic activity, caution will be thrown to the wind citing energy security, revenue collections and demand related reasons. We are not perfect at predicting earthquakes and this will feed in well coupled with the less urgent concern about future generations. Sentiments like *"If it has not yet happened, then it is not as much a problem"* are not rare with *"the now"* always taking precedence!

But here is another problem, plate tectonics on which our continents float are all connected in some way; so, having fracking East, West, North and South will only put us at greater risk of catastrophe. We are at the mercy of the earth's core, we are at the mercy of the convective currents and whichever directions the plates swing I hope we will have done our very best in optimizing this conundrum, a conundrum of clean energy security, and the growing threat that it will pose on the earth's crust and delicate water and soil ecosystem.

'We are at crossroads' has never been truer.

Blending Technology, Finance, and Policy to power the poor.

If water is life, then energy must be the means by which that life is lived. Yet for many communities both water and energy are hard to find. Trees are cut down to make charcoal for cooking; the resulting environmental destruction causes aridity manifested by drying of river streams further alienating communities at the bottom of the pyramid.

Poverty thrives in these circumstances, creating a viscous cycle for households that largely depend on subsistence production. Therefore, finding strategies to accelerate access to clean energy is a vital pillar for lifting the poverty burden off the shoulders of such communities.

According to the International Energy Agency (IEA), 1.4 Billion people do not have access to electricity, nearly a quarter of the world's population. Hart & Schneider (2010) make a distinction between the populations that have no access to energy from those that are forced to rely on traditional biomass sources due to the lack of clean and safe cooking fuels. The authors mention that 1.6 billion people fall in the category of lack of access to electricity, while the population relying on traditional biomass amount to 2 billion. This therefore points to a population of 3.6 billion people to be targeted with clean energy, since energy and climate are closely linked.

Blending *technology, finance, and policy* customized to the needs of poor communities might unlock the gateway to accelerated uptake of clean energy for close to one third of the world's population relegated to the Bottom of the Pyramid (BoP).

Technology.
Different communities have various resources, needs, and capabilities/strengths which technology ought to consider. Therefore, finding a fit within the country's infrastructure and the country's capacity is important. We should seek *efficient coupling* between local resources (solar, wind, biomass, or small hydro etc.) and needs (cooking, lighting, refrigeration, production) while preserving health and environment. We should also focus on technology solutions that *overcome any resource competition like* energy-water and energy-food competition.

Although Technology has advanced in providing clean energy solutions, it has left out poor communities that can hardly afford these solutions in countries whose policies do not reflect the energy challenges. Accelerating the adoption of clean energy is a *race against time* to minimize the hazard of continuous environmental degradation exacerbated by population increase.

Finance
Innovative business models that meet the needs of the poor are vital. For example, although solar panels are on sale in developing countries, uptake is still low due to high upfront cost, Inflexible payment schemes, and not least high cost of loan collection for micro-finance institutions. Sources of income for poor communities are sporadic and piecemeal, and therefore technology must match this financing characteristic. Some innovators are currently developing Pay-As-You-Go Solar solutions to mirror the earnings of poor communities. This is one of the reasons why communities use the kerosene lamp, because they can refill by

buying kerosene from the small rural shops. Therefore, it is important to seek new financing innovations and develop on existing best practice to tailor clean energy financing to the needs of BoP.

Policy

Finally, necessary policy interventions are needed to support propagating of clean energy in poor communities. Energy policies in most of the developing world have not yet been updated to reflect current energy needs and realities, especially regarding opportunities for clean energy. Standards on technology have not been set and this has resulted in poor quality solar panels being sold to price sensitive masses. The credibility of solar as a form of energy is hurt by the counterfeit solar panels, and this calls for standards in the market to protect these vulnerable communities from such predatory fraud. However, policy issues in developing countries are more complicated, for example there is a lack of coordination and symmetry between ministries yet for example the energy ministry and the environment ministry ought to work more closely. Not only is horizontal communication and coordination lacking, but vertical coordination is lacking between the ministries and other executive arms of the government. In the end this all makes implementation of much need policy intervention problematic.

Five forces for Energy 2050.

Much discussion has gone on in both academic and corporate boardrooms, on the triple bottom line being the solution to the energy 2050 challenge. Having listened to the pros and cons, I propose my five forces approach as the solution to the Energy supply challenge of 2050.

Building on the triple bottom line.

The triple bottom line proposes a balance between Social objectives, Environmental objectives, and financial objective. To a large
extent this has been useful to address the need for companies to
maintain shareholder value in the pursuit of social and environmental objectives. A project that tries to optimize the trio would
be ideal. I am full of gratitude for the contribution the model has
made toward better understanding of the Sustainability discussion. During my recent trip to Verona, Italy, I kept thinking about
this model, the culmination of which is my proposed "Five forces
for Energy 205."

Setbacks.

The major flaw in the triple bottom line emanates from within its
construction and assumptions. For example, some Environmental and social objectives if well executed could in the long or short
run result in benefits to the company that far outweigh any financial cash flow NPV requirements. Funding a project to plant trees
in the community, companies could exist in a cleaner atmosphere;
attract talent that is driven to work for higher goals. The absence
of measurement tools for social and environmental objectives
should not be used as a basis of requiring financial goals to be met.
We need to re-invent adequate measurement techniques to repre-
sent the benefits to shareholder value.

Requiring business decisions to pass the test of Social, Environmental, and Financial has the challenge of alienating projects
whose return enriches the corporate existence as a whole.

Decisions will vary from one individual to another; one company
to another, one country to another and the big question is "how
can we be sure we are making the right decision?".

Stakeholder engagement is the answer. The challenge is to define
the right set of stakeholders and attach the ideal priority and
begin the journey of charting their needs, and expectations to
position as an ideal citizen and custodian of shareholder wealth.

You may not get it right the first time, nor the second, this is a continuous work in progress. Through transparency your stakeholders can learn to trust the corporate activity.

The 'five forces of Energy 2050'

The two *additional* drivers or engines to improve the triple bottom line are: Innovation and Efficiency – *thus making them fourth and fifth force.*

To begin with efficiency, some companies are claiming to be 'green' when in fact their actions are purely about efficiency and minimizing resource wastage. This is not an invention but rather common age-old business practice. Examples include fitting energy saving light bulbs or printing less paper. Besides, the goal of the world's exponentially growing energy demand cannot be adequately solved by efficiency; Instead, Innovation is the right pony to put your bet on. The benefit of such a model is that it realigns business to move beyond regulatory compliance and 'green' marketing to focus on collectively achieving the 2050 energy challenge.

An additional benefit of five forces as opposed to bottom line is that it gives executives more options to value benefits that are beyond financial returns which could stifle greening industry.

Interpretation of Germany's Energy Approach.

With the help these three charts that I developed, energy analysts, policy makers, and investors can gain a fresh understanding of the key success drivers for the German Energy Efficiency (EE) and Renewable Energy (RE) approach. The question I aim to answer is regarding to the extent to which Germany's model can be replicated across borders.

In the first chart below, all the emissions reduction targets and accelerated adoption of Renewable energy (RE) are engulfed in the German Climate Policy which unlike for most countries operating 'switch on switch off' policies', Germany's is sustained over time. There is a sound regulatory environment (*e.g. Energy Conservation Act, Renewable Energy Sources Act*) and financial incentives oiling the three-pronged force of Energy Efficiency, Energy Saving and RE promotion.

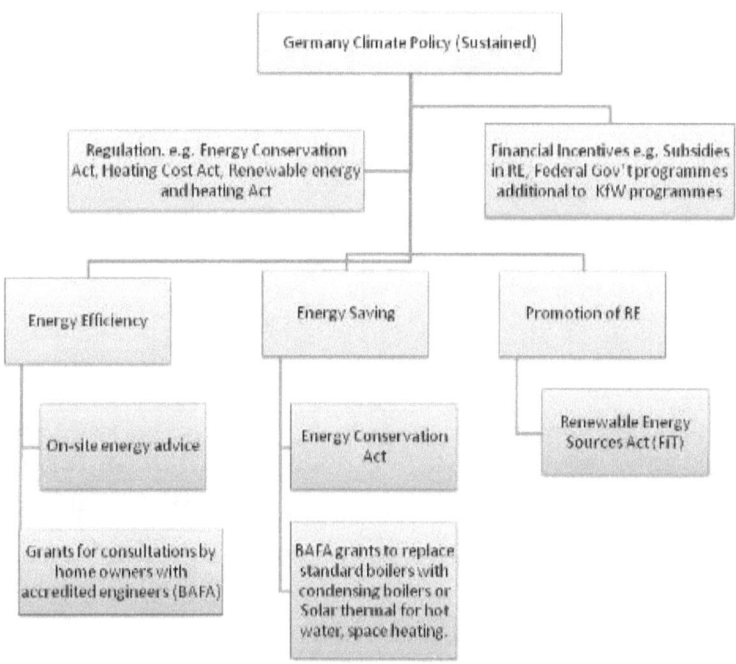

The second chart below reveals linkages between KfW Banken-gruppe, German Government, and the Market. This synchronized relationship is at the core of the emissions reduction in Germany to the extent that it enables low interest loans to be provided to engine the whole process. Do not ignore the fact that KfW using the AAA credit rating on the market has access to low interest funds, yet simultaneously benefiting from annual Federal Government funding to further lower the interest rate.

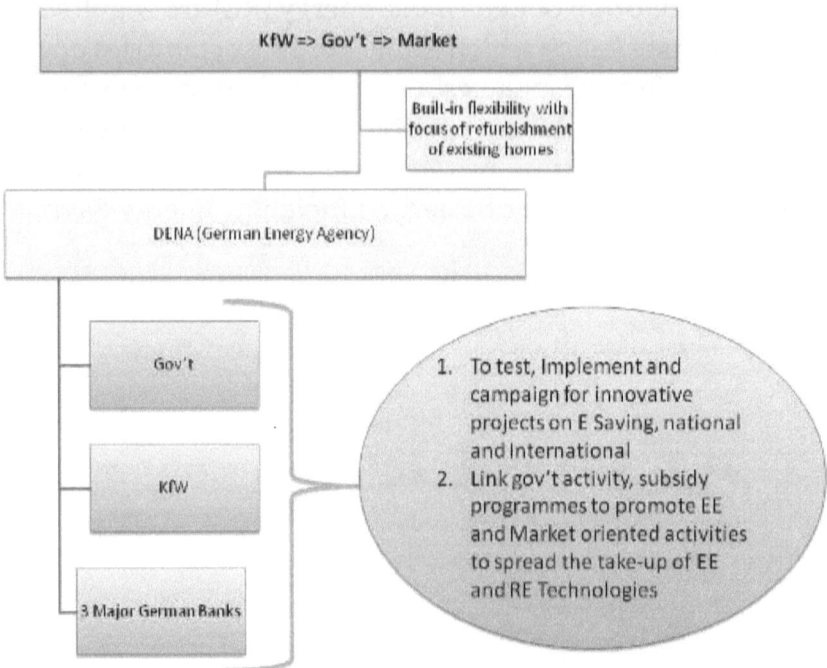

The third chart below narrowed down further to the KfW structure to gain an insight into the final trickledown effect. I dis-
covered that the Environment and climate protection division applied a combination of loans, grants, and special subsidies to drive
take-up in the market.

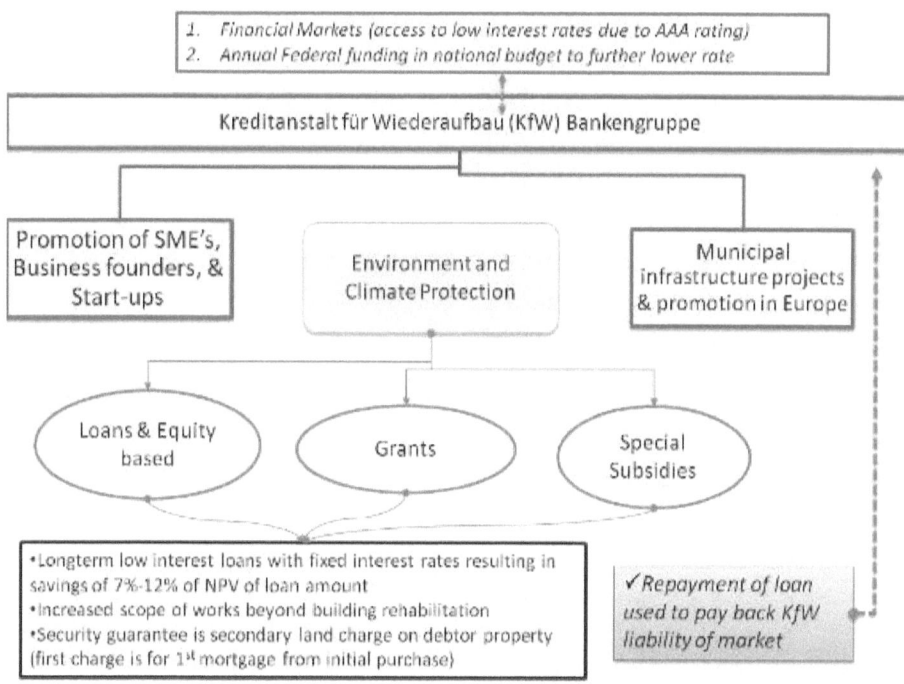

Finally, but very key is the information synergy not only within the various arms of the German structure but perhaps more importantly the synergy is through information sharing with the public, advice services given, even to the extent of covering the costs of expert energy efficiency assessments.

To answer the question of how the German model can be replicated elsewhere, I think the structures are easy to set-up; the hardest part of the replication/adaptation is the information sharing, trust and the will by the interested parties to make it work. This inertia could be the ultimate barrier to any fruitful learning and implementation.

How do you structure Green Deals?

It depends. The success of efforts to combat climate change will largely depend on the extent to which green projects can be profitable and realize returns for investors at the least risk possible. Even the most environmentally conscious investors need safe returns on green projects, along with the environment, and social benefits. For investors it is really having to satisfy the social, economic, and environmental objects simultaneously.

Then the question arises, how does one structure green deals that leave investors with an acceptable degree of comfort? A myriad of innovative sustainable projects in the energy sector have emerged, and although nothing is cut in stone, they reveal useful insights.

Demand with a local touch is king, but so is the source of investment.

The 2012 German – Swedish consortium that put up Eur200 million for MVV waste-to-energy plant in UK is a good example on how investors can reduce risk by guaranteeing demand. Well how did they do this? The Electricity and heat generated by the Thermal waste to energy plant was designed to be used primarily by a British naval base situated in Plymouth when it commences operations in 2014.

Beyond demand, one of the unique aspects in this project is that three UK regional authorities of Plymouth City Council, Devon County Council, and Torbay Council came together under the South West Devon Waste Partnership (SWDWP). This is significant because most municipalities world over might not be in position to singly solicit and manage these projects, with the solution requiring a of neighboring municipalities on one project.

Project details.

A consortium made up of KfW IPEX-Bank, a subsidiary of German development bank KfW Bankengruppe, and Swedish bank Svenska Handelsbanken designed a project to provide Eur200 million in project finance for a thermal waste-to-energy plant being built by Germany-based MVV Energie in Plymouth, England. The combined heat and power project was projected to cost a total of

Eur250 million, was contracted by the South West Devon Waste Partnership, which comprises three regional authorities that united for the project.

The plant forecasted an electrical capacity of up to 22.5 MW and a heat capacity of 23.3 MW. Each bank designed to provide an equal share of the finance. KfW's involvement is due not only to the presence of MVV subsidiary MVV Umwelt but also German firms Baumgarte Boiler Systems, Stuttgarter LAB, Imtech and SAR Electronic, all of which are supplying equipment for the plant.

Here below is diagram showing my interpretation of the project structure.

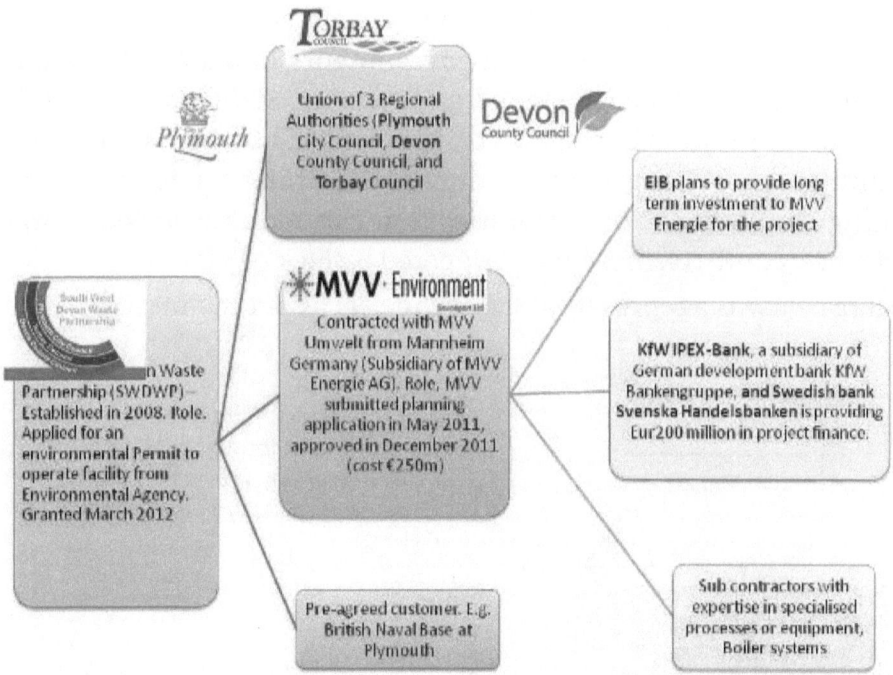

Expanding on already existing business by capitalizing on existing relationships with government.

For companies with a presence in Africa, Sustainability is an opportunity to expand their business profile without a sweat by building on already existing relationship with the respective governments. This is the step Siemens took in Nigeria by building on pre-existing oil and gas capacity in country when they launched their first venture in Nigeria for newly formed Solar and Hydro division. This is an example of a Private Finance Initiative (PFI). A PFI is a contract between a public body, and a private company. A PFI contract involves the private sector making capital investment in the assets required to deliver improved services. This is unlike a 'typical' outsourcing deal where the private sector organization only takes over the day to day operations, either renting or having been gifted the assets used in service delivery.

Project details.

Siemens and Nigerian Government agreed a series of Commercial-scale solar projects. The Local governments in Bauchi, Kano and Gombe in Nigeria each signed a MOU with Siemens to build 30 MW solar projects in their state. For Nigeria this being an opportunity to meet her growing energy needs whilst concurrently creating employment opportunities that can reduce the communal clashes, conflicts, insecurity triggered by lack of jobs.

Here below is a representation of the deal as per my interpreted.

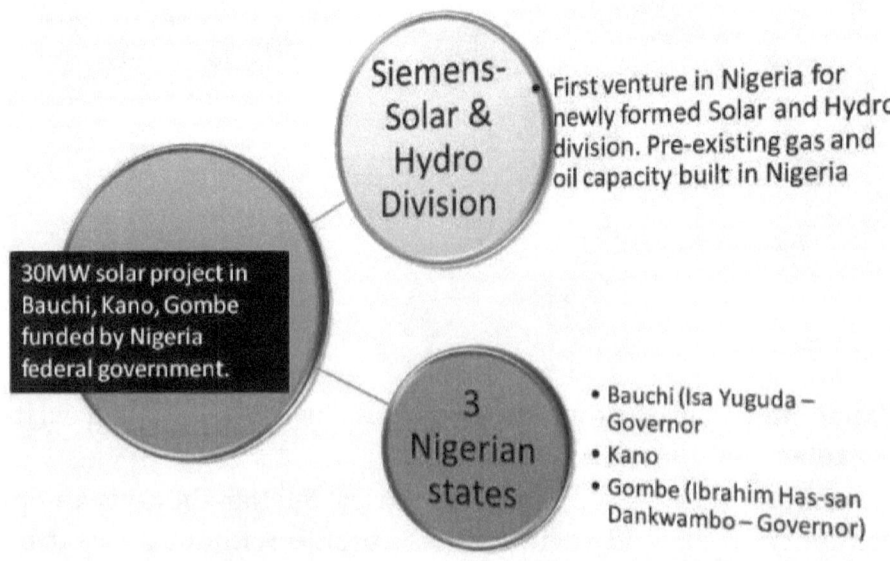

How governments world over stand to gain from Green deals.

Here below are five benefits governments stand to gain if they embrace green investment and energy efficiency.

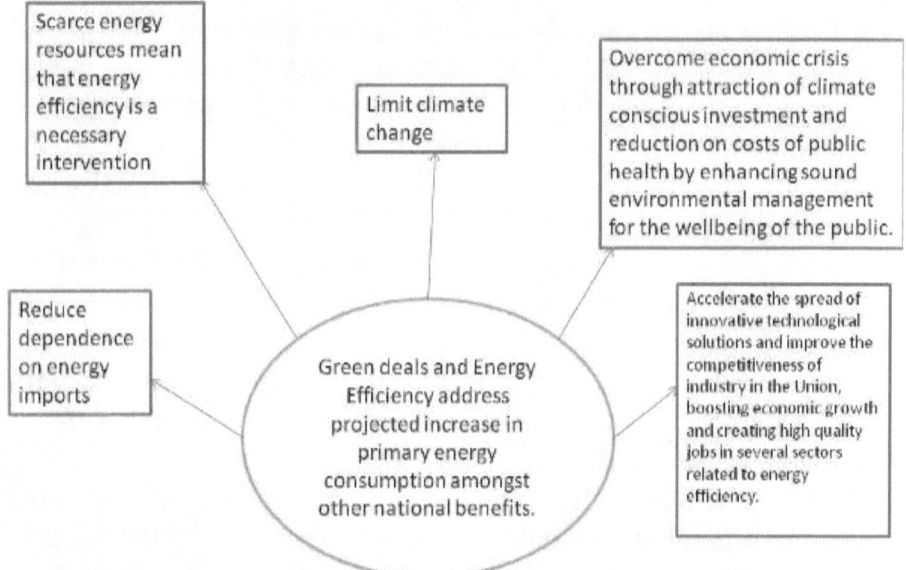

There is no rule of thumb as regards structuring green deals as the underlying conditions vary from one country to another, as well as from the resources, companies involved. What these examples show though, is that a great deal of innovation and flexibility is required. All these opportunities are time bound and to a large extent bare first mover advantages.

Financial Innovation accelerating
Energy Efficiency investment.

I was drawn to this discussion when faced with a recurring impasse in which households, industries and governments argue insufficiency of funds as the reason for low uptake of energy efficiency installations. And rightly so. Whilst these investments generate significant savings in energy costs, the initial capital expenditure required can often inhibit project development.

However, this need not be. Using innovative financial models, we can bypass this bottleneck and accelerate uptake of energy efficiency (EE) investments. To meet growing energy needs, energy efficiency is vital in addition to other interventions such as accelerated adoption of clean energy sources. Investment can also mean innovation, more so when saliently powerful bottlenecks inhibit adoption.

One such business model growing in popularity due to its benefits is termed 'Forfeiting Structure'. Most executives are not looking for in-depth knowledge of the so called "Forfeiting Structure" in energy efficiency financing, but just the fundamentals. As a result I prepared the key knowledge areas of the "Forfeiting Structure" in energy efficiency financing, as tools to improve the quality of decisions, EE pitch ability and necessary adjustments taking into account, corporate, national and regional conditions.

The representation below is my interpretation of the Energy Efficiency (EE) forfeiting mechanism.

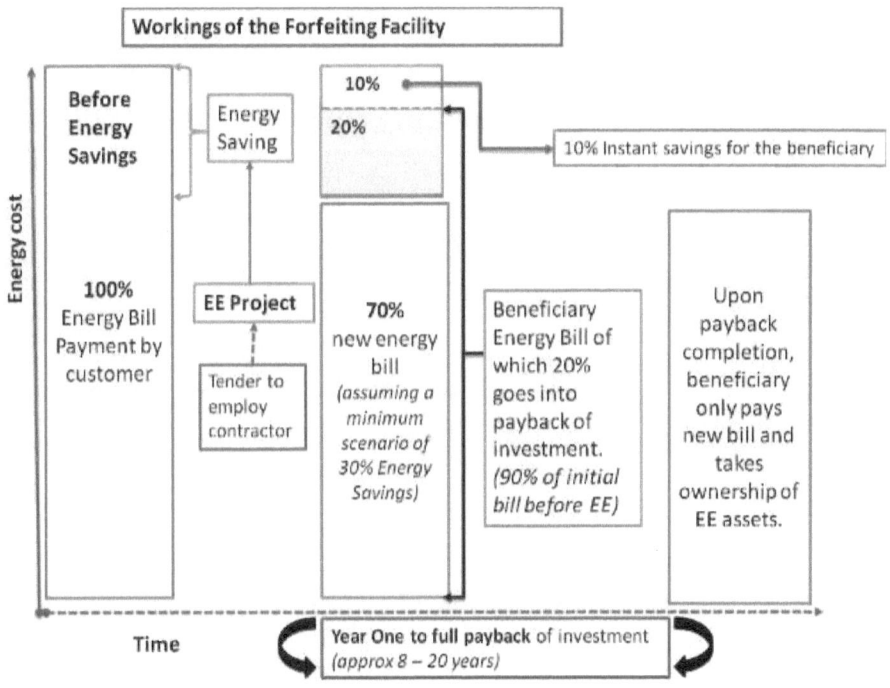

Under a forfeiting structure, the customer/beneficiary continues to pay either 100% or preferably 90% of the original bill – being the average of the previous three years. Energy Savings gained contribute to paying back the initial capital investment. At full pay back the beneficiary takes full ownership of the assets employed and pays the energy bill as-is (which is less the full energy savings).

Gap

Significant EE opportunities exist in various countries that could be tapped. Projects could include public lighting retrofit, municipal/public heating/cooling, among others.

However, these opportunities have not been fully explored due to the existing bottlenecks among which; the lack of buy-in by public authorities who do not anticipate the projected energy savings. Limitations in public funding, absence of strong base of energy savings companies (ESCOs).

Rationale for EE intervention. (A case for Jobs, Innovation, and low carbon Growth)

The rationale for EE is best illustrated using the European Directives 2004/8/EC & 2006/32/EC as summarized in the diagram below.

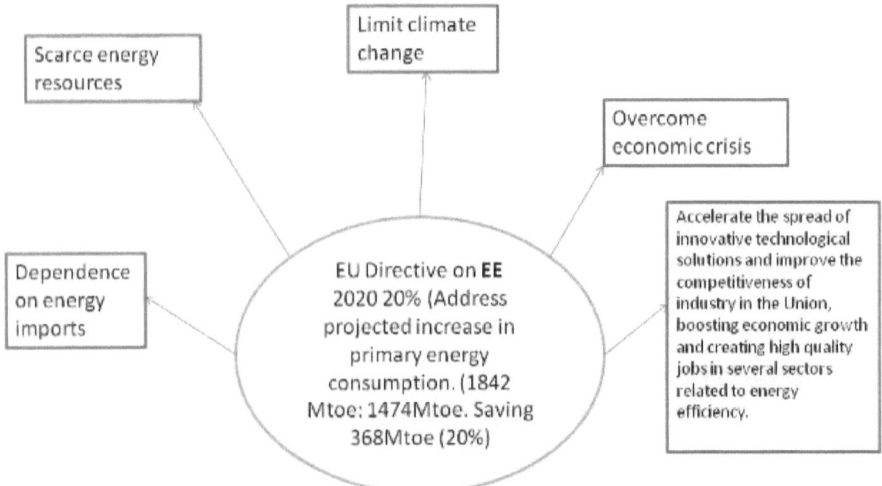

DIRECTIVE OF THE EUROPEAN PARLIAMENT AND OF THE COUNCIL on energy efficiency and repealing Directives 2004/8/EC and 2006/32/EC - 11th September 2012

Most countries are facing unprecedented challenges resulting from increased dependence on energy imports and scarce energy resources, and need to limit climate change, yet simultaneously overcome the prevailing economic crisis. Energy Efficiency (EE) is a valuable means to address these challenges by improving the security of supply through reduction of primary energy consumption and decreasing energy imports. EE reduces greenhouse gas emissions in a cost-effective way and thereby mitigating climate change.

Shifting to a more energy efficient economy should also accelerate the spread of innovative technologies and improve the competitiveness of industry, thus boosting economic growth and creating high quality jobs in several sectors.

Poem - Waiting for tomorrow is a luxury

How can we meet today's human needs without compromising the ability of future generations to meet theirs? Acting today and now is one way of addressing the problem. Daring to make steps today will get us started, and maybe we will be proven to have erred tomorrow, but tomorrow is a luxury we have not got.

Our ambition for energy is to make the small steps Today.

Today

Mine is a vain leap
The height is high, yet my sight departs not from the goal
Whence it takes me? I wonder
Possibility and impossibility merge into one
Neither encouraging my pursuit, nor rejecting it.
Which is the answer?
Time and urgency deny me a final look back
I pounce, I jump
I reach out for the goal
To secure energy supply for 2050
I haven't reached my goal
Thus I push the air left beneath my feet
In utter rejection of the status quo
I lengthen my reach, hoping this effort Today will make a difference
I do not only seek to try. I seek to try Today
And if tomorrow finds my effort inadequate

I shall boast in having acted Today,
Using Today's knowledge
Yet should you read this tomorrow
Know ye that tomorrow is a luxury which I never had.
For Today is my chance,
My moment, to leave the world better than I found it.
Today.

BY RONALD RWAKIGUMBA.

SUSTAINABLE DEVELOPMENT

'Sustainable development, far from being a new and restrictive condition to industrial and financial progress, provides the keys that will unlock all the major markets of the future.'

HNJ. SMITS

There are those who say the world needs to press a reset button, other who argue the reset button has already been set, in fact many reset buttons. One then wonders to which default settings the world wishes to reset. Could also reason that we cannot easily press the reset button if we have lost our compass. Unaware of where we are, we reset in vain. The initial steps perhaps to re-examine where we are and re-imagine a new world we wish to reset to.

Rather than be protagonists of the status quo in which pollution and resource consumption rise with economic growth, we should act as antagonists by promoting a disruptive model in which despite economic growth, resource extraction/consumption grows at a slower rate. This is what is referred to as a Green Industry.

Signs of resource strain were self-evident, and the idea of pending resource scarcity is increasingly being accepted by businesses that increasingly struggle to secure raw material inputs for production, and even when they secure them, it is likely to be at a higher price. Since the resource strain is felt at the industry level, a general price increase can be expected especially for essential commodities. A strategic shift could be for companies to enter their suppliers' markets to secure raw materials, but this also attracts new risks which they may not have the competence or advantage to manage.

For a short while prices for basic household goods like sugar might appear to reduce as has been the case in Uganda due to increased cultivation of sugarcanes, and introduction of new firms lowering prices in competitive regimes, however there is the danger of these gains being watered down by rise in food crop prices since fewer food crops are being grown with land use favoring sugarcane growing in some regions. Also given the unequivocal response to climate change it is highly likely that we will continue to experience extreme weather conditions such as severe droughts and floods.

Today, the very ecological balance pressures that caused our ancestors' migration are now coming back to challenge us, only this time, we have nowhere else to migrate to. Intra-Africa migrations as early as 1000 BC where caused by drought, famine, population increase, resource-based conflicts, epidemics/diseases. Today, East Africans face the same challenges which are now further fueled by climate change.

Universal Commonwealth
or the lack of.

Even with the World Trade Organization (WTO) reaching a first ever trade reform deal in Bali, international trade persists with market imperfections that continue to affect farmers and industries in developing countries. For example, India's food subsidies program means that farmers, traders, and industries in developing countries may never know the true price of rice from India which is lower than the cost of rice grown and produced locally. These subsidies are artificially driving crop prices and maintaining poverty in many developing countries which are highly dependent on agricultural sector.

Uganda is one example of high dependence on agriculture with 24pc and 23pc of GDP generated from Agriculture, forestry, and fishing in 2008, and 2009, respectively. Unable to compete in international markets amidst these unreal prices, the greatest impact is felt by small farmers who are forced to match these prices. One could argue that India's government has a duty to feed her poor and ensure. Ironically in the past India opposed agricultural subsidies in the US and EU in 2001 before growing their own agricultural subsidies along with Brazil, Russia, and China. Temporarily, these policies appear to help the developed and emerging markets at the expense of the developing nations, however, in the long run, the perpetuated poverty suffered by developing countries will diminish the export market volumes. The impoverished farmers who make the bulk of developing nations might not afford to buy even these cheaper imported food stuffs, which might in turn drive local governments to impose tariffs to adjust the market at the expense of interfering with a free market economic system.

This need not be. If countries like India embraced their global responsibility by gradually phasing out these subsidies, the potential of developing countries would be unlocked and in the long run even India would benefit through increased exports of various products to a population emerging out of poverty with increased purchasing power.

A salient observation is how developing countries are increasingly importing more from among themselves leveraging their respective comparative advantages. If they perceive to be getting less favorable deals from emerging markets, they will be incentivized to further increase economic cooperation among themselves. According to the Uganda Bureaus of Statistics, the country imported goods worth US $684 million in 2010 from India, having imported USD $521 million the previous year. Compare that with imports from China amounting to US$ 414 million and 379 million in 2010 and 2009, respectively. Putting this into perspective, combined imports from Germany, Italy, United Kingdom, Sweden, and other European countries to Uganda in 2010 were US $702 only US$ 72million more than India alone.

> *For the same period, Uganda imported goods worth 671 million and US $657 million from the COMESA (Common Markets for Eastern and Southern Africa) region in 2010 and 2009, respectively. The trade with East and Southern Africa is nearly equal to that with all European countries combined, or India, and is now greater than the imports from China.*

The implication being that, although developing countries are looking to emerging markets like China and India for good trade terms, developing nations are increasingly cooperating amongst each other to boost trade between developing nations. The resultant effect is clear, for emerging and developed states should seek to lift off the burdens on developing nations whose growth also benefits them.

Although China is now the second most vital economy in the world, her international trade activities have not reflected this. To date Chinese companies are aggressively competing with local companies in developing markets in low value and low premium commodities. The low prices of Chinese commodities make it near impossible for local industries to compete. Ironically, even South Africa which under the BRICS trade block is supposed to cooperate with China finds herself out competed by China in major African

Markets.

On the policy level, China is committed to assisting developing countries come out of poverty with numerous aid and infrastructure development projects; however, it remains counterproductive that Chinese firms using the power of their low price goods drives local industries to closure. China needs to revise how it now engages with developing countries to achieve her policy objective of contributing to poverty reduction in present day developing states. Sub Saharan Africa is now growing at faster GDP growth rate, BRICS are cooling with slowing GDP growth than projected, further evidencing that a truly sustainable economic growth model takes on a global perspective or is otherwise temporary at best.

Can individual nations achieve sustainable development without global sustainable development? The answer is 'no' since in the long-term, for nations to do well, their neighbors also ought to fair well, the entire world needs to be well. Sustainable economic growth for all nations therefore requires that countries look beyond their individual borders and analyze the impact their policies have on the entire globe and seek an optimum that would result in humanity, as a whole, being better off.

The case for a multi-sectoral integrated approach

I am standing half distance up Eifel tower. It is obvious there is an unusual glow on my face, a kind of glow that only comes when you see something or someone you longed for. I know it because earlier on a bus in Greece from Athens International Airport Eleftherios Venizelos, I saw a vacationer headed to Thesalonika glow almost as though she could light a dark room. I looked at her several times and eventually told her there was a glow on her face. She told me she knew and even lit the more when she saw the white bricked houses along the wayside.

Still by the Paris' Eifel tower, a fellow tourist offered to take my picture, the first shot did not go right, and the second was perfect, so she said. Little did she know my mind had travelled six thousand miles to Uganda where Sustainable development is very much a fight from within and without. I come from the Kingdom of Tooro in Western Uganda bordering DR Congo and to address the bottlenecks of Sustainable Development I seek to evaluate the tradeoffs that existed and how our choices caused my village more harm.

Connecting Water, Health, Education, and Poverty.
We had two main sources of water for my village in Kijanju, Kabarole municipality, comprising: a little stream, and a pond. Not too long after 1993 our stream dried out and could no longer support the community, leaving the pond as the only source of water in the proximity. At this point we should have questioned the circumstances that led to the stream drying out, but for the most part we did not. There were a few murmurs that the pursuit for good crop had motivated farming of vegetables closer and closer to the stream to tap underground water. There was also increased deforestation for construction of houses to accommodate the growing population. Today, the pond does not exist anymore, and you would be beleaguered to find a person who recalls the well.

My community is now relying on piped water and rainfall harvesting. For communities that still largely live below a dollar a day, the costs of buying piped water are inhibitive. Instead they send the young lads to distant valleys in search of the last sanctuaries of naturally flowing water. Of course, most of this water is not clean and brings diseases into homes, homes that cannot afford medical costs. The cycle is so vicious because the young lads do not do their schoolwork and miss the benefit a good education could provide in breaking this cycle of poverty. Due to these conditions most boys drop out of school to find jobs to support their families, and the girls are married off young to fetch bride price. The jobs for the boys involve brick making, construction, animal rearing, and cultivation, among others. The Ministry of Education in Uganda has noted that that most girls dropout of school because of early pregnancies further fueling families not to support girl child education.

It is all connected, and it is for this reason that I believe in a holistic approach to development, especially regarding poverty eradication. Fixing one thing alone will not get us to our desired destination because these issues are intertwined and require a multifaceted approach.

As the sun was setting, I and my colleagues would be tying our bundles of firewood from Kinyamasika forest ready to walk toward the horizon knowing that dinner would be cooked and weary that we had not even started our school work due the next day. And when darkness descended on my village, it was time to light a little paraffin fueled lamp known locally as 'Tadoba'. It comprises a thread which dips on one end into a metallic container containing paraffin and is lit on the other end.

Connecting Energy, Health, Education, and Environment.

I will admit, for young lads, firewood was fun to collect. It was a good excuse to be away from home and gave us a chance to swim in the rainwater-filled cement dugouts as we chatted. On an unproductive day, a colleague could chip in a few sticks of firewood to make your bundle bigger and the favor would be returned the following day and vice versa. We gradually moved from picking dry wood to climbing trees using ropes to reach giant stems as firewood became scarcer and scarcer to find. In fact, such was the depletion of the forest in Kinyamasika that we were banned from going there to collect firewood by the authorities at Virika Parish. Little did we know that this was all part of a bigger danger to the community.

When the wood reached home, our sisters cooked the food in a soot filled kitchen that was no doubt a hazard to their health. As we had to interchangeably share the only Tadoba between the kitchen and doing schoolwork, I rapidly scribbled away the home-work. So, I was not surprised when my grades at Buhinga Primary School in Fort Portal plummeted.

Connecting Poverty, Environment, Technology and Security.

The reason often given for cutting down trees is more complicated than it appears. Some studies have shown that the money fre-quently spent on refilling the Tadoba with paraffin is cumulatively more, compared to acquiring a solar panel. With the introduction of a tax on paraffin in Uganda's budget of 2013/2014, alternative energies are poised to reach parity. However, the challenge for communities is having to come up with a lump-sum of money to cover the one-off cost of the solar panels. I think this leaves a challenge to micro-finance institutions to extent credit facilities to cover this gap. The credibility of solar as a form of energy is hurt by the counterfeit solar panels that take advantage of the price sensitive masses. This calls for standards in the market to protect these vulnerable communities from such predatory fraud.

Technology combined with innovative business models is making strides to match the needs of these communities, for example some companies are pioneering *'Pay as you go'* solar applications. This is particularly useful because it mirrors the piecemeal earn-ing of the communities and helps overcome the burden of having to come up with huge sums of money at once. It also mirrors the Paraffin refill costs thus accelerating the switch to cleaner fuels.

Insecurity is tightly coupled with environmental hazards with bitter fights with displaced communities demanding to relocate to the Queen Elizabeth National Park after their homes were flooded. There have already been killings of elephants and other wild animals as farmers encroach on land demarcated for wild animals. In Kenya deadly tribal fights center on resource use strained exacerbated by environmental degradation are frequent occurences. One wonders whether the renewed attacks on gorillas and their caretakers in Rwanda is also another resource driven conflict.

It is all connected and embracing a holistic and integrated development approach is key. It is obvious health, environment, energy, education, security, and economic growth are intertwined and as such demand a corresponding multisectoral response. The Sustainability Development Goals torch that path; a path I wish had come sooner. Godspeed.

Wildlife-human resource strain

Not long ago, on an ordinary afternoon driving from Kampala to Fort Portal in Uganda, a giant elephant sped across the road with barely meters or seconds from impact. With the highway surrounded by bushes I had no way of anticipating the elephant and was only lucky that it crossed very fast and never changed course. With drought reducing food and water sources for animals, and with humans encroaching to wildlife parks for settlement a wildlife-human resource competition is inevitable. Elephants are now resorting to encroaching on farmer's crops for food putting beast and man in a battle for resources. If elephants could speak, the story would be different, because according to the Uganda Wildlife Authority, it is us who through encroachment have forced the cordial coexistence of humankind and beast to result in confrontation.

The same could be said to the battle between the people in Mayuge district with crocodiles for limited resources, land, and water impacting many families whose loved ones and domestic animals have been needlessly lost or maimed. Given the resource efficiency trends over the last 30 years; Resource scarcity is already putting a strain on business-as-usual and this has increased the prices of inputs/raw materials. With competition it is difficult for companies to pass all the increments to customers in form of higher prices thus likely to result in more efficiency. However, this will only result in resource exploitation.

In part, this is due to exponential population growth. Only fifty years ago, Uganda's population was just 8 million in 1962, but with a high total fertility rate of 6.2 children, her population has since increased to over 34 and 42 million in 2012 and 2020 respectively with more than half the population (56%) below 18years.

It is not only population, which is causing severe resource depletion, but also Product lifecycle challenges.

> The developing nations which are poised to increase consumption even further are also characterized with the least infrastructure to facilitate cradle to cradle production. This is a pending challenge which should be solved in its infancy. The costs and carbon footprint of returning 'goods-in-their-final-life' to developed countries present yet another inhibition. Efficiency could reduce the rate of resource extraction through recycling of products at the end of their useful life.

There is that potential for innovation to come to our rescue. I think that would be a great thing if it happens, however I consider resource efficiency an insurance policy just in case the innovation does not happen in good time. Something about innovation that is peculiar, for investors to back a new technology, they ask for only 'proven' technology, 'profile' of inventors, proven background of developing innovation…. the list is long. It is a harsh status quo given that existing technologies also took time to mature into dominant proven uses.

Costs and Constraints of energy conversion? For people to move from cooking using firewood to cleaner sources like natural gas, they are in effect moving from a 'free' source of energy to one they have to pay for, if the distance traveled and time spent collecting firewood are not costed. To appreciate the vagueness associated with a migration to cleaner energy sources, let us take a former classmate, Moses who took on the challenge of charcoal by working with a network of female entrepreneurs to commercialize briquette. The briquettes can be used not only for cookin, but the residue also used as fertilizers, all at a cost 20% cheaper than charcoal from trees. Other salient benefits of briquettes include employment given to youth, and women. The conversion costs to cleaner sources are vague since in pursing sustainability significant benefits are realized save for the sacrifice and risk entrepreneurs undertake.

The constraints are the resources with which we apply to production, yet these very constraints have a positive effect in producing innovation and adaptability as we strive to acknowledge them so as to achieve welfare improvement, a balance and mind-shift.

Rather than nature being our constraint, it is our inability to look and consider the long-term, which was and still is our true constraint. Our constraints are many and sustainability is part of the solution and not the constraint. The alternative to sustainability is dire; we could get used to living with wild animals.

Is it Developing Countries' turn to Pollute?

Often, I encounter the question of whether developing countries can afford sustainability. In fact, a few years ago academics argued that poor countries should be allowed to pollute as much as they want because the developed world had to first pollute during the industrial age to reach developed status.

Quite common to encounter statements like

> *'The rich countries are rich because they industrialized but they had an advantage which less developed countries don't.'*

Resources are finite and to maximize gains developing countries should be more efficient in resource use for longevity which makes industrialization (*as we know it today*) is not enviable. Instead 'Green Industrialization' offers more benefits. The developing world has a chance to grow and develop differently, smartly not only because it is good for the environment but great for economic reasons emanating from resource efficiency gains. This dual potential is essentially one about the economy because climate induced destruction and losses risk slowing or rescinding development gains Floods and drought are becoming commonplace with heightening severity in Mozambique, Kenya, Uganda, and Somalia, yet scientist predict even worse climatic events if the status quo of environment degradation persists unabated.

Aggregated, developing nations have a strong impetus to promote green industry by encouraging efficient resource use and reduction in pollution to facilitate a development whose growth does not necessarily result in rampant pollution or excessive resource extraction. Besides, the costs of correcting an unsustainable system far outweigh the cost of being sustainable from the outset. For example, large cities like Beijing, Mexico face a huge task of investing in improving the quality of air.

The costs associated with transitioning developing countries to be sustainable can be shouldered in-part through the Clean Development Mechanism (CDM) among other interventions.

The concept of greening industries facilitates the desired sustainable economic growth as developing nations accelerate adoption of modern farming methods that are more drought resistant and improve the quality of products to boost export revenues. By inculcating a system of resource efficiency throughout the supply chain and minimize pollution hazards, developing nations can truly decouple, or at least reduce the rate at which resource extraction/consumption grows with economic growth. This Green Industrialization is Africa's opportunity which developed countries missed in the industrial age.

Redefining Waste

Instantly, I get shocked when I encounter definitions of waste as '*a pejorative term for unwanted materials.*' Only to be calmed later by the additional text that '*The term can be described as subjective and inaccurate because waste to one person is not waste to another.*' Nonetheless this points to society's general perception of waste. Given definition of waste influences the framework of resource use and management, a framework that begins with growing demand, and management of finite resources in a world, perhaps worth examining the definition further.

In the summer of 2013, I met Massimo Calzati, an Engineer focusing on eco-sphere friendly projects in the energy sector but also with implications on efficiency through material recycling. I have my friend Silvia to thank for this meeting which she setup during her work in Bio energy at Massimo's firm Studio Ecoingegneri. Massimo explained that the rationale of this new definition of '*waste*' is that the material or energy outputs of human activities may be classified as either '*product*' or '*waste*', regardless of their environmental or health impact ("footprint"). He also goes on to explain that *both 'product' and 'waste' are strictly economic categories.*

There may be products carrying highly negative environmental and/or health impact and, conversely, wastes carrying low impact. These impacts should be somehow quantitatively evaluated to be reflected in the economic cost of a product or waste. This evaluation is one of the most difficult – yet inescapable – task economic and environmental scientists have for the future. Businesses are expected and/or required to manage their waste for environmental/efficiency purposes, and thus the meaning of waste guides them in meeting or exceeding these expectations and/or rules.

Directive 2008/98/EC of The European Parliament and of The Council defines waste as;

> *'any substance or object which the holder discards or intends or is required to discard'*

This definition is both subjective and ambiguous, and mainly talks about what the holder does with waste. Massimo Calzati proposes an alternative new definition that talks about waste with notes to explain terms used as follows.

Definition by Massimo.

> *The output (of either material or energy kind) of a human activity is defined as "waste" when either of the following circumstances occur:*

> *1) it leaves the "Techno-sphere" and is delivered to the Eco-sphere as a result of an intentional choice of that who holds it, or because, for any*

reason, it is impossible to use it as an input to any human activity, including the one which produced it;

2) it remains within the "Techno-sphere" in as much it is delivered to a human activity of a particular kind, its unique function being that of mitigating and possibly eliminating the negative impacts which would derive to either human or environmental health and integrity from direct introduction of the output into the Eco-sphere.

Notes.

The expression *"human activity"* is here used to identify any process, introduced by Mankind (i.e. not spontaneously present in Nature), through which given results (outputs), of either material or energy kind, are obtained, starting from given resources (inputs), of either material or energy kind.

Inputs to a human activity may consist of primary natural resources or output results of other human activities. The interconnection of all human activities forms a system which can be identified as *"Techno-sphere"* as opposed to the "Eco-sphere", the latter being the interconnected systems of all natural subsystems providing primary resources and ecological services – or, in simpler words, the natural environment.

Today, it is certain that this eco-sphere is both endangered, and ailing, owing to the cumulative effects of human activity or *'techno-sphere'*. The clarity, specificity of this definition would enable businesses to track their environmental footprint with a higher degree of certainty.

It is a win-win situation – even for businesses as they highly rely on scarce resources to profitably produce goods. Also, in their best interest to mitigate adverse effects of pollution. If this seems a daunting task, remember Hearn Lafcadio, who said that

'all good work is done the way ants do things, little by little.'

How to Green a Country,
Lessons from Uganda.

Sir Winston Churchill on visiting the source of the River Nile in Jinja, Uganda, and the vast enrichment of flora and fauna across this country, famously described Uganda as *'The Pearl of Africa'*.

Greening Industry is a practical presentation of the key hallmarks of enabling sustainable development in a manner that developing countries like Uganda can implement. A Green Industry is one of efficient resource use and reduction in pollution to facilitate a kind of development whose growth does not necessarily result in rampant pollution or excessive resource extraction.

The government of Uganda has adopted various policy tools through various ministries which not only strengthen competitiveness and efficiency of industry but also address social-economic challenges of unemployment, pollution, access to energy.

Below are specific policies/programs which have been implemented, guided by a 'green' Energy Policy.

ONE VILLAGE ONE PRODUCT (OVOP) Program.
Introduced in 2008 under the Ministry of Trade, Industry and Cooperatives, the One Village one Product (OVOP) program set out to promote economic use of resources and increase incomes through value addition to local resources, human capital development and marketing of products and services. Value Addition processes have the potential to unlock a myriad of challenges such as creation of employment, generation of export earnings. Packaging & Labeling is one way the program seeks to promote products.

Resource efficiency is a cornerstone of this program because it emphasizes competitiveness of the products on the international market. Entrepreneurs are encouraged to make products that are competitive in terms of international standards, but also ensure efficiency to breakeven. One of the challenges faced by the program like insufficient production of primary products for processing, could act as another motivation to aggressively pursue innovative resource efficiency practice. Some of the challenges faced include limited access to financial resources, inadequate skills in business, and production, and limited market linkages for their products.

Moving forward, more emphasis could be placed on the encouraging cradle to cradle production in which the products can still find use when they reach the so-called end of their useful life.

UGANDA'S ENERGY POLICY UGANDA. Uganda's Energy Policy (2002) acknowledges the need to maintain a balance with the environment and social aspects, as it states that

> 'Energy development and environmental damage are intricately related. The policy recognizes the need to mitigate both the physical and social environmental impacts created by energy development, especially hydropower.'

In fact, the policy goal is 'To meet the energy needs of Uganda's population for social and economic development in an environmentally sustainable manner'.

Uganda completed an inventory of its greenhouse gas emissions to meet its commitments as a signatory to the United Nations Climate Change Convention (UNCCC). Several initiatives to conserve biomass resources have been undertaken Government and the private sector, including NGOs. They include the promotion of improved stoves, as well as afforestation. However, even the Ministry acknowledges that the impact of these efforts is still limited. Government is implementing a Solar PV pilot project through a financing mechanism that makes it possible for both PV consumers and vendors to obtain credit from banks for solar rural electrification. A national biomass energy demand strategy was developed for the period 2001-2010 so as to mitigate the hazardous impact which can arise for uncontrolled deforestation for firewood, by synchronizing the energy strategies in the energy policy, the national forest plan and the national environment plan.

However, continued use of Charcoal remains a challenge for Uganda as fuelwood has contributed to the degradation of the environment, not to mention the health hazards from the soot.

Energy Efficiency (EE) is far from full potential, significant energy saving opportunities still remain especially in the transport sector, and one way of promoting energy efficiency is by promoting companies and industry to establish energy management systems with a goal of reaching ISO 50001 compliance.

Uganda needs to develop a reliable railway network to reduce on transport related pollution. The market of Energy Savings Companies (ESCOs) is still in infancy and the Ministry of Energy and Mineral Development should device incentives and resource capacity development to cultivate these players.

ENVIRONMENT AND NATURAL RESOURCES. The environment of Uganda is under threat from natural and man-made drivers of change including poverty, rapid population growth, urbanization, agricultural expansion, Informal settlement development, industrialization, and the impacts of climate variability, among others.

To protect the environment, the following actions have been taken by the Ministry of Water and Environment.

Wetland Boundary Demarcation Strategy resulted in a total of 443.4km in 16 districts of wetland demarcated in 16 districts to avoid encroachment

Natural regeneration was achieved through eviction of encroachers and this resulted in a total of 2,079.4 hectares of degraded section of 8 wetlands being restored.

Compliance monitoring and Enforcement strategy measure was put in place to ensure that proposed developments in or near wetland systems comply with the legal regime. Training of 150 staff from Environment Protection Police Unit was also conducted.

ENHANCING AGRICULTURAL PRODUCTION AND PRODUCTIVITY.

The biggest weakness and the ultimate cause of household poverty in Uganda to having a large fraction of the population engage in subsistence agricultural production with little to no household income generated from agriculture. The government acknowledges this and promotes commercializing agriculture noting that

> 'whereas it was enough to engage in agriculture for food production and consumption yesterday the modern population needs to do farming for food and as well as an economic activity from which it can derive monetary gain in order to eradicate household poverty.'

The National Development Plan identifies agriculture as a vital contributory growth sector capable of reducing poverty and stimulating economic growth.

Government efforts include:

Provision of affordable finance to enable farmers acquire necessary infrastructure to promote transformation to commercial agricultural production. Eligible projects are financed at a preferential interest rate, about half of that applied by commercial banks.

Presidential Initiative on Banana Industrial Development (PIBID) was set up to reduce wastage in bananas, support development of innovative solutions to promote efficiency thus reinforcing Uganda's food security. Wastage is because the banana was only eaten as a direct food. According to estimates, over 10 million tones are produced each year.

The PIBID has registered a Banana brand, not only in the region, but also across the world called, 'Tooke' which means Banana. The flour (Tooke), has been tested against international quality standards in Germany and France, is now being promoted throughout Uganda and is being used in bread, cakes, biscuits, and other processed products, including baby food. It is hoped that 'Tooke' products will also prove successful in export markets.

Recommendations on Greening Uganda. On a national policy level, the government needs to:

Establish a common understanding across government organs of the need to promote efficient resource use emanating and minimize pollution, stemming from the top leadership.

There is need to streamline policies to minimize overlap and avoid conflicting programs between various organs/ministries. Closely related, the government needs to promote Horizontal/ and vertical communication within the ministry. This is because Green Industry challenges, solutions cut across various ministries and thus needs a solution to mirror this

Encourage Public Private Partnerships (PPP) to bolster needs such as finance for example in creating energy efficiency capacity, investment in new technology.

Innovation need to be supported especially at resource extraction and disposal to find ways of closing the production loop or pursuing industrial ecology.

Not least, Government needs to promote Information Communication Technology (ICT) especially in local rural areas to provide useful information exchange and bridge the gap between the producers and the market, so as to address one of the challenges Identified was due to limited market linkages.

The concept of greening a country facilitates the desired sustainable economic growth. The risks in pursuing a path of business as usual are self-evident. Uganda needs to accelerate adoption of modern farming methods that are more drought resistant and improve the quality of our products to boost export revenues. Uganda's successes and challenges in Greening the nation provide practical guides and learnings for other countries as they design their path to a sustainable future for generations present and to come.

East Africa, hurdles on the path to Sustainable Development.

Kenya.
In 1969 there were only 10.9 million Kenyans. By 2009 the population of Kenya was 38.6 million. Meaning the population grew by 28 million in just 40 years. At this rate by 2050 the population will have reached close to 65 million.

This would not be a challenge if the population were planned for with adequate employment and living means for the population. The Kenya 2009 MDG annual report shows that only 2 million people are formally employed, with 8 million in informal employment. With most of the population younger than 25, social tensions are likely increase fueled by unemployment.

The strain of rapid population growth is reflected in the tribal clashes in the Tana River region with conflict being over land and water rights. In January 2013 eight people died when raiders from the Pokomo community attacked an Orma community village, with the Pokomo being farmers, while the Orma raise cattle. The same year at least 20 people were killed, and more than 15 others got injured in fresh inter-clan clashes in the northern Kenyan border town of Moyale, Marsabit County between Borana and Gabra communities near the border with Ethiopia. Again, strained resources: water and grazing land are that core of the conflict, and these resources are further diminishing owing to a changing climate.

Kenya is prone to disasters, especially in the arid and semi-arid land areas. Drought is the most prevalent natural hazard. Kenya's droughts in April 2003 left 62 dead and almost 90,000 displaced by floods. Earlier in March, floods in Kenya killed 74 people, with 99,043 others displaced. To protect the environment, the link between access to energy and the environment cannot be ignored. Lack of access to energy, such as electricity, results in people cutting down trees, leading to environmental degradation.

Climate change mitigation, adaptation, and use of modern farming methods will be critical for Kenya toward realizing Sustainable development.

Rwanda

The National Institute of Statistics of Rwanda enumerates the population of Rwanda at 10,537,222 people in 2012. Ten years earlier Rwanda's population was 8,128,553 people in 2002. A year later, in 2013 the population is 11.46 million as per World Bank data. At this rate, Rwanda will constitute over 20 million people, for the same resource.

Yet Rwanda faces another hidden challenge; Rural – Urban Migration. Statistics provided by Rwanda's National Institute of Statistics show that Kigali, the capital city had 765,325 people in 2002, but by 2012 Kigali was populated to a tune of 1,135,428 people, a growth of 48%. If there is not enough employment in the urban areas, with an effect on the food security of the country since there will be fewer hands in food growing areas to cultivate.

According to the Rwanda MDG Country report 2007, by 2006,

56.9% of Rwandans were still below the national poverty line, an improvement from 60% six years earlier in 2000. Here is the paradox, for the same period Rwanda was growing at a GDP growth rate of 9.4%, while poverty reduction was happening at a rate of 1%. This remains a challenge for East African countries as a whole; we boast about GDP but do not translate that growth into poverty reduction. We have no excuses because in 1990 Sub-Saharan Africa was at the same poverty level of 56% as East Asia and Pacific, by 2010 East Asia only had 12.5% of population below $1.25 while Sub-Saharan Africa had 48.5% still below the poverty line. These statistics are contained in the MDG report of 2013.

Rwanda has made significant strides in reducing Infant motility from 86 deaths per 1,000 live births in 2006 to 38 deaths per 1,000 live births in 2011. Rwanda is now the safest place for infants to be born in East Africa as per world bank figures, with Uganda, Tanzania, Kenya, Burundi at 58, 45,48, 86 deaths per 1,000 live births, respectively.

Burundi is the riskiest place for children to be born. Put in context Colombia, Chile, China, Canada, Botswana, and Brazil combined still have a lower infant mortality rate, that is, 75 deaths per 1000 live births. Contrast that with Burundi's 86 deaths per 1000 lives.

Tanzania.

It was safer for mothers to deliver children in 1990 than 2008. The plight of mothers in Tanzania rather than improve only got worse. According to Tanzania MDG report 2008, the maternal mortality rate in Tanzania was 529 deaths per 1000 live births in 1990. Eighteen years later in 2008, the maternal mortality rate was 578 deaths per 1000 live births. One of the drivers was because fewer births were attended by skilled health personnel since by 2008 only 63% of Births in Tanzania were attended by skilled health personnel.

Access to potable water remains a challenge for rural Tanzanians. According to the Tanzania MDG report 2008 51% of rural population had access to potable water in 1990, 18 years later still only

57.1% of the rural population have access to potable water.

Uganda

Uganda seems to be moving in two opposite directions, on the one hand caring about reconciling economic, environment, and social tensions sustainably, on the other focusing on satisfying each tension separately and not simultaneously. When it comes to promising investments that jeopardize the environment, the government seems less interested in the eco-system concerns, narrowly focusing on industrialization. This has been subject to several demonstrations in the past regarding Mabira forest industrial development plans or dam constructions. In most cases protest have had a positive impact in either halting the projects or making sure more environmental impact assessments are conducted.

Projected to exceed 80 million by 2050, Uganda's population was just 8 million in 1962, but with a total fertility rate of 6.2 children, her population has since increased to over 40 million by 2020.

Uganda's total labor force increased from 10.9 million people in 2005/2006 to 13.4 million people in 2009/2010, as per statistics form Uganda's Population Secretariat. Therefore, it comes as no surprise that unemployment rate was 9.5% for urban areas with 3.0% in rural areas.

With 66% of Uganda's population engaged in agriculture, climatic changes have severely affected the earnings and livelihood of communities most of which depend on subsistence forms of agriculture. Evidence of Subsistence cultivation is shown by the fact that the National Land cover of cultivated land increased from 84,010.0sq km in 1990 to 99,018.4sq km in 2005. This was without any significant change in commercial farmlands which remained at 684.5sq km from 1990, to 2000 and up to 2005. As per 2009/2010 statistics 24.5% of Ugandan's still live below a dollar a day and this constituted 7.5 million people. Regionally 24.5% is good compared to Rwanda's 56.9%, or Tanzania's 33.64%.

Just like in Rwanda the mismatch exists between the rate of poverty reduction and the rate of economic growth. Economic growth is happening without nearly equivocal reduction in poverty. In short, the poor are seeing very little of the national economic growth.

As a result, the scale of resource extraction has increased, environmental degradation has grown, industrial pollution is largely unchecked, to such an extent that we cannot afford the path of business as usual. Why so? Because developing countries like Uganda heavily need efficient resource use to ensure that the path of development we started continues. We need to have more control of our climate and weather by safeguarding the delicate eco-balance and avoid exceeding the carrying capacity of fragile nature. The reason nature is fragile, is that we rarely do the additions and the changes which appear slight in the short-term are not only devastating in the long run but also more difficult and expensive to reverse, if at all.

To support this population growth Uganda needs to accelerate adoption of modern farming methods that are more drought resistant and improve the quality of products to boost export revenues. For continuity we need to inculcate a system of resource efficiency throughout the supply chain and minimize pollution hazards. This way we can truly decouple, or at least reduce the rate at which resource extraction/consumption grows with economic growth.

The East African region does have the solutions, and they are the right fixes, but not without challenges such as weak synchronization, coordination, and consistency.

We need to ensure horizontal and vertical integration of government programs across various ministries and within ministries. We are notorious for running switch-on switch-off kind of responses. That would not be a problem if the programs were self-sustaining, but even then, basic monitoring and evaluation is required.

Countries like Germany have succeed in building climate change resilience by ensuring programs are sustained over time within a sound regulatory environment (e.g. Energy Conservation Act, Renewable Energy Sources Act) all with good synchronization not only within the government, but also between the government and the market.

Solutions we have, if only the will.

Growth Elasticity of Poverty

African countries have been growing at a relatively fast rate since the beginning of the new millennium. In fact, over the period 2001–2008, Africa was among the fastest growing continents. Despite the progress that has been made over the last decade, the current pattern of growth is neither inclusive nor sustainable.

Evidence of this is contained in the Millennium Development Goals 2013 report which shows that although East Asia and Africa both experienced economic growth, for East Asia that growth highly translated into poverty reduction, much unlike in Sub-Saharan Africa due to its lower *growth elasticity of poverty (GEP)* which measures the extent to which economic growth contributes to poverty reduction. Table 2 in the report (*Regional breakdown of poverty incidence (1990-2010) and projections for 2015*) reveals that

> 56pc of people in East Asia and Sub-Saharan Africa were poor in 1990. Twenty years later in 2010, East Asia and the Pacific only had 12.5% poor: in stark contrast to Sub-Saharan Africa's 48% poor.

Although the share of the world's population living in extreme poverty declined from 15.7 per cent in 2010 to 10.0 per cent in 2015. However, the pace of global poverty reduction has been decelerating. Nowcast estimates put the global poverty rate in 2019 at 8.2 per cent. This is according to the 2020 Sustainable Development Goals Report released by the United Nations. Findings indicate that while the world was already off-track to end poverty by 2030, the negative impacts posed by the Covid-19 pandemic exacerbated the poverty gap as described below;

> "Forecasts indicate that the pandemic will push 71 million people back into extreme poverty in 2020, in what would be the first rise in global poverty since 1998. Many of these people are workers in the informal economy, whose incomes dropped by 60 per cent in the first month of the crisis. Half of the global workforce – 1.6 billion people – support themselves and their families through insecure and often unsafe jobs in the informal economy, and have been significantly affected."

Africa's dependence on resources is obvious, what is less obvious though is the exportation of value to industrialized countries, and the inefficiency in raw material extraction, processing, and use.

Resource efficiency must be accompanied by value addition processes which will create jobs and maximize revenue generation through export of finished products.

Beyond a closed-loop production. Cradle to Cradle production is not the epitome of supply chain efficiency, the apex is called Industrial Ecology (A system of systems). To understand Industrial Ecology, imagine various companies in each industry all aiming for sustainability and cradle to cradle production. Now imagine all those companies in an industry coming together to achieve sustainability of the industry and not merely of their individual firms. Now this is a merging of systems, thus Industrial Ecology is also described as a system of systems.

Perhaps even industrial ecology might not be the epitome, because it is worth considering a system-of-systems of systems. Meaning that industries (system of systems) could come together depending on their linkages, geographical or otherwise and aim for efficiency

At the conclusion of a visit in Le Marche, Italy, a wine producing gentleman stressed to me that he and his peers do not need any luck, having achieved prosperity, his future and that of his peers is secure. It is us the youth, he said, that need to be wished luck, it is the youth, he said, who are *in bocca de lupo* (in the mouth of the wolf) and therefore need to *crepi il lupo* (kill the wolf), it is also the youth who are bearing the burden of worsening unsustainable growth.

Story - Lampedusa is only a Tip of the Iceberg.

On 3 October 2013, a boat carrying migrants from Libya to Italy sank off the Italian island of Lampedusa killing more than over 360 people. I was awoken at 2:30am by flashbacks of images of over 360 coffins lined up awaiting funeral. Various leaders who have visited the island have voiced how they may never forget what they saw, a monument sculpture of an open door called La Porta d'Europa - the door of Europe was dedicated in Lampedusa to the migrants who died.

Lampedusa sadly seems only the tip of a very large iceberg. Underneath Africa's glorious economic growth is over 40 percent of the population in chronic poverty which fuels the desperate journeys migrants make across the Mediterranean. So desperate that the threat of death by drowning as they cross to Europe, is insufficient to deter their pursuit.

There is hope, and then dashed hopes. Since 2013 many more dangerous voyages have been made across the same waters with over 19,000 reported missing or dead by 2019, averaging over 3,000 deaths/missing per year in the six years leading to 2019. Sadly, incidents like Lampedusa have not deter migrants from seeking the promise of Camelot in Europe, perhaps because the worst has already happened to them; they are already staring into a bleak unending future.

Policing the Mediterranean is merely treating the symptom, the real disease is poverty, which a more inclusive growth that increases concurrently with reduction in poverty could alleviate. There are many coffins that go unnoticed because they are not lined up together. For example, as per 2012 statistics five hundred people mostly children die daily from Malaria alone in Kenya, Uganda, and Tanzania combined.

Entrepreneurship is a good place to start finding solutions. There is a misconception that entrepreneurship is last resort for reducing youth unemployment. There is more, as it is key to growing nations, and prospering citizens. Entrepreneurship is not merely a fix to the unemployment problem, but also the opportunity arising from the problem.

Fair enough, entrepreneurship reduces unemployment, however more importantly, entrepreneurs breathe new life in the world economies by making obsolete the present inefficient processes and birthing a new sustainable world.

High population growth rates in developing countries creating a largely young schooled, and at times, very well-schooled but unemployed population is another danger to lookout for. It is still early enough to impart technical skills among the youth in wood and metal works, brick making etc. to generate vital sources of livelihood.

Government programs to finance the youth are highly politicized, plagued by corruption, and inefficiently disbursed. There have been efforts by a few governments to train the youth to impart business skills, however, the business plans of the youth also need help. Beyond training, youth need to be mentored and guided on generating value and capturing it if the rate of failing start-ups is to be reduced.

Universities have a particularly vital role to play to cover up for the inefficiencies of government. They can start with choice of courses taught, by inculcating entrepreneurial modules with practical focus of students seeking market opportunities to explore. Throughout the progression of their courses, they can be encouraged to develop and refine their business ideas further. But this too faces the problem of inability of academic oriented lectures to suitable guide students in market-based offerings. Therefore, even the Universities cannot do it on their own; Businesses could volunteer their industry expertise to complement the academia with practical market skills to drive business ideas to fruition. But they face a problem of preying on ideas of the aspiring entrepreneurs. (right safeguards)

The obstacles to entrepreneurship that remain are very welcome, as a true test of the grit of young people since, staying power is needed in running and sustaining a business. The Chinese will tell you that

'One step at a time is good walking'

for C. S. Lewis *'What saves a man is to take a step. Then another step.'* Aspiring entrepreneurs will profit from Ruth Stafford Peale's advice as they make those first steps *'find a need and fill it.'*
May we be equal to the task.

Story - From dolls to water tanks

Yuko, also locally known as Nakamya while in Uganda volunteered at a regional hospital having left Hokkaido district in Northern Japan. During her free time, she assisted a primary school and Health Center II acquire water tanks for rainwater harvesting to improve sanitation.

However, it was her later project with women in Kitenga that captivated me the most. Call it a match made in heaven and you will not be further from the truth. When Yuko visited Kitenga subcounty in Mubende, Uganda and found village people using dirty water, she knew she had to also assist this community to have a water tank to access clean water.

A Kairos moment occurred when Yuko met a lady making dolls for children, and it occurred to her that if more women participated in making these dolls, they would be able to sell them in Japan and raise money for a water tank. But there were a few challenges, dolls in Japan were preferred in small sizes and this required assisting the women to start making smaller dolls to suite the Japanese market. Five women were soon all trained and able to make these local crafts to be exported to Hokkaido at a price of $4 each to raise money to acquire their water tank.

Yuko's mother Mari was also eager to help using her experience in not only making crafts but also her knowledge of the local crafts market in Japan, Mari helped Yuko and the village women by coordinating the sale of the Ugandan crafts in Japan.

In total the Kitenga pump project will cost USD1,600. Having already raised USD$1,420, Yuko is now preparing another batch of 100 dolls heading to Japan to be able to raise the remaining amount.

When I met Yuko I found her putting tags on the dolls in Japanese language with a little inscription of the purpose at the back.

113

To further reduce the project's carbon footprint, Yuko uses paper made from banana fiber which is locally produced in Uganda.

It is now obvious that the women of Kitenga will have their tank with construction. In a few days Yuko together with the women will begin procuring the materials necessary for not only the tank but also the brick barrier wall that will surround the tank and other peripherals.

The efforts by Yuko, her mother – Mari, and the hardworking women of Kitenga are testimony to the fact that we are one humanity, and sometimes we only need to work with local resources to generate the change we desire in the world.

There is no single story. There are many stories that can be told. Chimamanda Adichie, a great Author of our time puts perfectly when she says,

> *'Stories matter, many stories matter... and when we realize that there is never a single story we regain a kind of paradise.'*

ABOUT THE AUTHOR

Ronald Rwakigumba

An accidental author, Ronald immersed himself in everything sustainability while pursuing the Università di Bologna, Green Energy and Sustainable Businesses MBA.

This sparked more inquiry leading him on a path to learn, experience, and meet various experts & thinkers to unpack the people-planet-profit triple bottom line. His Financial Services, FMCG Marketing, and Educational Publishing private sector background created an invaluable experience for later initiatives promoting the Sustainable Development Goals.

A native of Uganda, Ronald is currently contributing toward bridging the humanitarian-development-peace triple nexus.